BE ANGRY, BUT DON'T BLOW IT!

Maintaining Your Passion Without Losing Your Cool

LISA BEVERE

THOMAS NELSON

Since 1798

NASHVILLE   DALLAS   MEXICO CITY   RIO DE JANEIRO

Published in Nashville, Tennessee, by Thomas Nelson.
Thomas Nelson is a registered trademark of Thomas Nelson, Inc.

Thomas Nelson, Inc. titles may be purchased in bulk for educational,
business, fund-raising, or sales promotional use. For information,
please e-mail SpecialMarkets@ThomasNelson.com.

Scripture quotations noted NKJV are from the NEW KING JAMES VERSION
of the Bible. © 1979, 1980, 1982, Thomas Nelson, Inc., Publishers.

Scripture quotations noted NASB are from the NEW AMERICAN
STANDARD BIBLE®. © The Lockman Foundation 1960, 1962, 1963,
1968, 1971, 1972, 1973, 1975, 1977. Used by permission.

Scripture quotations noted NIV are from the HOLY BIBLE: NEW
INTERNATIONAL VERSION®. © 1973, 1978, 1984 by International Bible Society.
Used by permission of Zondervan Publishing House. All rights reserved.

Scripture quotations noted KJV are from the KING JAMES VERSION.

Scripture quotations noted TEV are from Today's English Version.
© American Bible Society 1966, 1971, 1976, 1992.

Library of Congress Cataloging-in-Publication Data
Bevere, Lisa.
    Be angry, but don't blow it : maintaining your passion without losing your cool /
Lisa Bevere.
        p. cm.
    ISBN: 978-0-7852-6988-5 (pbk.)
    ISBN: 978-0-7852-8918-0 (repack)
    1. Christian women—Religious life. 2. Anger—Religious aspects—Christianity.
I. Title.
BV4527.B493 2000
248.8'43—dc21

                                                        00-035504
                                                        CIP

Printed in the United States of America
13 14 15 QG 987 6

*To all of those who have hurt the
ones they love and wish they hadn't . . . we have
the promise of hope and a new beginning.*

*To the many women whose hearts
have been touched by this book, thank you.*

"I have never read a book that spoke to me so clearly and personally. I have struggled all my life with anger and have been through counseling to help me forgive others for past hurts, but I have never had someone explain it the way you have."

"WOW! You sure know how to package this message in truth, transparency, and love. I could feel the presence of God while reading this book."

"I feel like the woman at the well-it is as if God is speaking to me directly through your book."

"I must say this book was unbelievable! I finally see there is hope for me after a childhood marked by abuse and abandonment."

"Thank you for being so transparent. You have helped set many captives free . . . including me!"

"After reading this book and applying it to my life, I can say I am a different person. This has affected my life more than I was ever expecting."

"I have now forgiven everyone who has ever wronged me. Great healing is taking place. Thank you so much for being open and sharing your life!"

Other Books by Lisa Bevere:

Kissed the Girls and Made Them Cry
Out of Control and Loving It!
The True Measure of a Woman
You Are Not What You Weigh

Books by John Bevere

A Heart Ablaze
The Bait of Satan
The Bait of Satan Study Guide
Breaking Intimidation
The Devil's Door
The Fear of the Lord
Thus Saith the Lord?
Under Cover
Victory in the Wilderness
The Voice of One Crying

CONTENTS

ACKNOWLEDGMENTS

My deepest appreciation and thanks to Victor Oliver and Cindy Blades for your gracious support and patience throughout this project.

To my precious boys: You are each such a gift from God. May you always maintain your passion without losing your cool. I love each of you more than words can say.

John: You have always been so understanding and supportive. You have been a faithful and true friend to me. You have wounded me with the truth and restored me with your love.

Jesus, when I am weak You are truly strong. Thank You for turning areas of tragedy in my life into triumphs. You have taken my darkness and turned it to light. I am eternally grateful.

Foreword

You may have heard the old proverb "Physician, heal yourself." Too often individuals try to teach a lifestyle they themselves do not live. Perhaps it is not an issue they have faced, or perhaps it is a truth only they know in theory but have yet to put into practice. Therefore, they may share a freedom they know is available but have yet to exercise.

Then there are others who teach from the perspective of coping with shortcomings. The problem is calmed but the root remains. So in essence the best hope we're offered is the management of sin. Yet God never intended for us to coexist with sin, but to be free from it.

I can honestly say, Lisa is one who both believes in and has been changed by the power of the gospel. We have been married for almost eighteen years, and you will see, by her openness in this book, that she definitely had a problem with rage. It was so forceful at times . . . it was frightening.

Lisa goes over specifics in her book, but I am here to confirm that she is a totally changed woman, and for more than ten years now, life has been different. I live with her, and if her change was not genuine, I would be the first to know. Yet I can honestly say that from the day her eyes were opened until now she has never had another outburst of wrath. I have watched her mettle tested in the fire of very difficult situations, ones that would have easily upset others who didn't even have a history of rage. I have personally witnessed the power of God working in her life. This change did not take place in a service or deliverance meeting, but in her own time of prayer. Out of this God has given her a message that carries not only great hope, but also true freedom. Scripture declares, "My people have gone into captivity, because they have no knowledge" (Isa. 5:13 NKJV). You hold in your hands a treasury of knowledge derived from God's Word. What God has done for Lisa, He longs to do for you.

I love Lisa and have great respect for her. She is my very best friend, but what stands far above even our close relationship as husband and wife is her genuine love for the Lord. She is a true disciple of the Lord Jesus Christ.

May God open your eyes in understanding as you read this book, and may the very same grace bring freedom to your life as well.

John Bevere
Author/Speaker
Colorado Springs, Colorado
January 2000

1 Broken Windows

The year was 1988 and John and I were in a heated discussion. So heated, in fact, I had ceased to speak. After clamping my mouth firmly shut for fear of what might come out, I turned my back to John and frantically threw myself into drying the dishes. I could feel my temperature rising as my breathing became deeper and more obvious until it sounded similar to what I had experienced during my labor. I had to stay in control. I couldn't allow the boiling torrent of angry words to gush unrestrained from my lips and drown my husband—no matter how upset I was with him.

John saw my silence from a very different perspective, though. He felt I was serving him the dreaded silent treatment. So he tried to draw me out of it with different forms of persuasion. When these failed he tried provocation.

All of a sudden it worked. I looked down at the plate in my hand. It was an unbreakable salad plate. As if in slow motion, I pivoted like a skilled discus thrower and released the plate. I watched helplessly as it flew through the air, wondering how it had become airborne and wishing I could somehow snatch it back. It glided purposefully and directly for my husband's head. John ducked to one side, escaping what appeared to be potential decapitation, and the plate soared on in an arc. Now it was far beyond the breakfast bar, where John stood in shock, and continued without wavering to span the length of the living room. *Could it possibly be gaining speed?* I wondered. I knew I couldn't even throw a Frisbee, yet here it was, sailing smoothly through the air without even a wobble.

The sound of breaking glass snapped me back to reality. I stared in disbelief at our picture window, which was now anything but one. It was a frame holding broken glass. I had missed the bottom part that held the screen and shattered the entire upper panel of glass. There was a moment of silence as we both stared at the window.

John was the first to break the silence. "I can't believe you threw that plate at me."

I had to agree. I found it hard to believe as well. But I obviously had, and it was done now.

We both moved cautiously toward the broken window. The cool January wind blew in to greet us. Down below our second floor apartment, lying motionless on the grass, was a lone white plate.

"I'll go get it," I muttered.

I slipped on my shoes and cautiously opened our door, hoping none of our neighbors had observed my outburst. The gusting Florida wind whipped my hair against my face. I slithered down the stairs, looking both ways, before I crept onto the common lawn. The plate was surrounded by slivers of broken glass from the window above. I glanced up to see if John or anyone else happened to be watching from their windows, but all I saw were reflections of a gray, dim sky. I brushed off the plate and snatched it close as I ran up the stairway between the buildings that now seemed more like a wind tunnel. I felt as if the wind itself were accusing me. It knew the truth, and I welcomed its harsh condemnation. I deserved it.

Again inside I looked at John. "I got the plate . . . it's not broken," I offered, holding it up for him to see as if it was some sort of consolation.

"You know I am going to tell them the truth, Lisa," he quietly assured me. "I am going to have to call maintenance and tell them my wife threw a plate at me, missed, and broke the window."

I nodded passively. All the rage was gone and only shame remained. "I know you will, but I am not going to be here when you tell them. I'm going to the store, so go ahead and call them now."

The silence was heavy and unnerving in contrast to the loud and heated exchange of words just a few moments before. I was amazed our sweet two-year-old son had slept through all of it. I hurried away from the scene of the crime.

Alone in our car I heaved a heavy sigh of desperation. As I turned the ignition, Christian worship music

> ✦ *All the rage was gone and only shame remained.*

filled the silence, but it seemed hollow and not for me. I turned it off and let the stillness shroud me again. I didn't want anything to comfort or console me. I wanted harsh reality. I pulled out of the driveway and decided to drive for a while before going to the store. I didn't want to chance a meeting with the maintenance man. What would he think? Here stands the next Lizzy Borden, a future ax murderer.

I decided to entertain shame and guilt as a form of punishment. I began to imagine the absolutely worst possible consequences. Perhaps a newspaper headline would be in order: "Youth Pastor's Enraged Wife Breaks Window at Local Apartment Complex." Would my husband be fired because of my behavior? Or even worse, what if it extended beyond John and me? What if the media seized the opportunity to denounce the Christian population of Orlando?

I didn't feel I had the right to pray God would somehow intervene on my behalf to cover this whole thing, but perhaps He would on behalf of the Christian community. I began to intercede on their behalf.

"Please God, for the sake of my church, the youth group, my husband, and all the Christians in Orlando, please do something. Nothing is too difficult for You. I know I don't deserve this intervention; don't do it for me, do it for everyone else!" I pleaded repeatedly.

I was honestly terrified the vivid images of my wild imagination might become painful realities. I imagined my next walk down the aisle of the church. I could almost see the disappointed looks and pointing fingers. I guessed at the whispers of shock as well as the knowing nods of others. "I always knew she had a problem with anger . . . the Spirit showed me," women would assure one another. Perhaps I would need to apologize to the entire congregation. Yet I feared my shame would still remain. How would my new friends look at me? Surely they would turn away from me. I imagined their husbands warning them in the privacy of their bedrooms to stay away from me. After all, the Bible warns us not to associate with an angry man—how much more an angry pastor's wife?

Hot tears now streaked my face. I stopped the car and composed myself before I went into the store. Surely there was no escape from what I had done. My husband wouldn't lie, and I didn't want him to. Maybe it wouldn't make the cover of the Orlando paper, but some consequence was inevitable. I resigned myself to this and admitted I deserved to suffer some sort of something. I only hoped I could recover from it when it was all over.

I found it hard to shop. I couldn't even remember what we really needed. I wandered aimlessly through the store. Our food budget was so tight, I did not have the liberty of purchasing food I already had or did not need. I wished I had made a shopping list. I felt like my head was in a fog. I managed to grab the few items I was certain we needed and headed back to the solitude of the car. The sun was setting now. Perhaps I could creep back in under a cover of darkness. I drove home and sat in the car for a while, watching for anyone leaving our apartment building. It was nearly six o'clock when I realized the maintenance man was probably off duty.

I grabbed the groceries and headed up the stairs. I knocked, then opened the unlocked door. I immediately noticed the plastic covering the gaping window; it billowed in and out as if it were breathing. I looked for John, dreading whatever he might tell me but ready to hear it nevertheless.

"What did he say?" I asked tentatively.

"All I can say is that God must really love you or you must have really prayed," John said, but there was no smile on his face.

"Why, what happened?" I probed.

"Well, I told you I was going to tell the truth," John began, "but it was really weird. When the maintenance guy came, Addison was at the door to greet him. He walked over to the sofa and pulled it forward from the window. He said, 'Wow, what happened here?' Then he bent over and put his hand up. 'Say no more,' he said, holding out a metal car of our son's. 'I have a two-year-old myself. We will replace the window tomorrow free of charge.' I started to say something but he stopped me again. 'Don't worry . . . this stuff happens. Just put up some plastic to keep out the bugs.' And he was out the door. I think he was in a hurry to go home for the night."

I sat down in shock. Was it possible that God had done this for me? No, He had done it for all the other reasons. Whatever the reason, it was now over and done with. My two-year-old son had taken the rap for the window. I began to feel the shame lift from my shoulders. I wasn't sure whether to laugh or cry with relief. None of my fears would become a reality.

I apologized again to my husband. But I have to admit, that night as I lay in bed I wondered if maybe God had covered me since my husband was not willing to. After all, John shouldn't have provoked me. It wasn't as if I broke windows every day. It was an isolated incident. God had forgiven me, or He wouldn't have covered it so amazingly. I shouldn't have thrown the plate . . . but John shouldn't have pushed me into it. I followed this line of reasoning until I fell asleep under the blanket of self-justification and righteousness. Gone was my repentance. Yes I would be more careful in the future . . . but, so should John.

I had reasoned away a valuable lesson. It would be more than a year before my anger would cost me enough to seek true repentance.

A CRY FOR HELP

Perhaps you have never broken a physical window. But there is a trail of shattered dreams and relationships. The mere fact you now hold this book means you're searching for the right balance in your life. You want to live a passionate yet godly life. Maybe you don't vent your rage—maybe you hold it in. It is still a source of destruction . . . self-destruction. Maybe you feel as though you are a habitation of broken windows. Angry bricks have been thrown and the cold winds have blown through and extinguished your passion and hope. I believe there is healing available for you.

Anger in and of itself is not wrong, but rage and fury escalate it into the dimension of the destructive. It is in the shadow and shame of this that we cry out for help. It is my prayer that you will somehow learn from my mistakes and grow to another level in your relationships, first with God and then with others.

> ✍ *Anger in and of itself is not wrong, but rage and fury escalate it into the dimension of the destructive.*

✍ *Heavenly Father,*

I come to You in the precious name of Jesus. Lord, mend the broken windows of my life. I am more interested in truth than appearances. I want the light of Your Word to search my heart and to know me. I want truth in my innermost being. I want to walk in freedom free from shame and guilt. Lord, instruct me in Your ways that I might walk in them. Pour out Your love that covers. Empower me with Your grace to submit to the truths that will set me free and allow You to be glorified in every area of my life.

2 Be Angry and Sin Not

The first part of Ephesians 4:26 is easy enough: *Be angry*. Most of us can accomplish this without even trying. It happens without warning. Someone cuts us off on the highway and careless words are hurled into the air, never to be retrieved. But more about that later. This verse seems at first a contradiction. It clearly grants us the right to feel anger. *Be angry*. There is not even a preceding disclaimer, like "If you absolutely have to get angry, then okay . . . be angry." Just a simple *Be angry*. The NIV translation reads, "In your anger do not sin." It seems to further validate the experience of anger, assuring us there will be times of anger, but telling us not to sin during them.

THE EMOTION OF ANGER

God gives us permission to be angry. He knows and understands man's inborn capacity for anger. It is an emotion He also is familiar with. It is recognized in the frustrated cry of the smallest infant as well as the patriot's outcry against injustice. It is heard in the agonized weeping of parents who grieve over the lost life of a child and the silent tremor of a grieving grandparent.

Anger is as valid a human emotion as joy, sorrow, faith, and fear. God tells us, *Be angry*, because it is okay to be upset. Even God gets angry—as a matter of fact, quite frequently. He was repeatedly angry with His chosen people. The Old Testament records several hundred references of His anger with Israel and other nations.

When an emotion is suppressed because it is not validated, it will eventually be expressed inappropriately. Conversely, if an emotion is expressed without restraint then sin will follow upon its heels. God Himself validates human anger. Yet most of us do not even understand anger. Is it throwing things and yelling and screaming at our loved ones? Is it holding a grudge over treacherous treatment? No, these are examples of inappropriate expressions of anger. There is a fine line between anger and sin.

> _God gives us permission to be angry._

The American Heritage Dictionary defines _anger_ as "strong usually temporary displeasure without specifying manner of expression."

It is okay to feel intense or strong displeasure over an event or at someone's actions. Displeasure encompasses disapproval, dislike, and annoyance. These feelings are common to all of us and may be daily occurrences. This definition of _anger_ does not provide a specific outlet or manner for the expression of anger. I believe this is because there are varied appropriate reactions and recourses to the corresponding offense. The responses would also vary with individual factors, such as age, personality, position, and place. Much more is expected of an adult in public than of a toddler. Likewise, the expectation is greater of those in authority or leadership. Authority figures shouldn't use position to vent their emotions or further their agendas. It is important for them to distance themselves from any personal offense long enough to become conscious of how it might affect those under their care or guidance.

For example, when I was a young, single heathen girl, I was quite vocal when it came to other drivers who offended me. I would volunteer my rating of their driving ability punctuated with a collection of explicit and colorful words. Then I became a Christian and learned the power of my words, how they bless or curse others. I also had the experience of being in a car with a godly woman when someone suddenly cut her off. I glanced over, watching for her response. She didn't cuss or even frown but gently smiled and waved as though to invite them to cut her off again. She turned to me with the comment, "We'll just sow a seed of kindness."

I tried to immediately pattern some of her behavior . . . well, at least I stopped cussing and yelling out the window. I still tended to grit my teeth and say things like, "Come on, sweetheart. I don't have all day. Pull out there . . . no one's going to hurt you!" I was given to honking instructively (for the safety of others of course). Then I became married with children.

I was no longer as comfortable talking to cars that couldn't hear me. Especially when I noticed my sweet sons following suit. They had taken up the defense of their mother against wayward drivers. They put on their best grumpy faces and yelled from their car seats in the backseat, then glanced forward for my approval. "He needs to learn how to drive! Right, Mom?" they'd cheer triumphantly.

Oops! Now my displeasure needed a different avenue of expression. It now affected and influenced others. My

> ✎ *When an emotion is suppressed because it is not validated, it will eventually be expressed inappropriately.*

little ones were copying me, and I no longer enjoyed the privilege of yelling at strangers (if it ever truly was mine in the first place). For the future safety and sanity of my children I needed to model constructive displeasure. I had to develop defensive rather than offensive driving skills. Now, instead of attacking the other drivers verbally, I try to teach my children, what was unsafe about their driving and how to respond to it. When a semi is barreling down on me, I say something like, "Maybe this guy is upset or in a hurry.

We'll just get out of his way." Then I change lanes. I have to admit, though, I still do not invite others to cut me off.

TEMPORARY ANGER

Let's look again at the definition of *anger:* "strong usually temporary displeasure without specifying manner of expression." It encompasses the word *temporary*, which means "momentary, passing, short-lived, or fleeting." Therefore, anger by definition should be brief and transitory, not drawn out and dangerous. Too frequently we live in a constant state of flare-up punctuated by brief interludes of happiness. God models the healthy type of anger for us: "For his anger lasts only a moment, but his favor lasts a lifetime" (Ps. 30:5 NIV).

The ratio of anger to favor is very low. David described God's anger as lasting but a moment. David should know; he experienced the anger of the Lord first-hand. He lost his son when the anger of the Lord was kindled against his secret sins of adultery and murder. David could have become

> *Too frequently we live in a constant state of flare-up punctuated by brief interludes of happiness.*

embittered against God and viewed His anger as lasting a lifetime and His favor as momentary. Did not the sword continually visit his house? Yet David had caught a glimpse of God's character and nature. Through repentance he clung to God's loving-kindness and mercy.

God in His anger may temporarily turn His face away, but by way of resolvement not by way of rejection. He understands our need to look away or walk away from the source of displeasure to prevent a destructive venting of anger. We do not walk away from others to punish them; we turn away so the embers of anger can cool and reason can again rule our hearts.

10

God told Israel: "Go up to the land flowing with milk and honey. But I will not go with you, because you are a stiff-necked people and I might destroy you on the way" (Ex. 33:3 NIV). And also: "For a small moment have I forsaken thee; but with great mercies will I gather thee" (Isa. 54:7 KJV).

He forsakes or turns away for but a *small* moment then returns to gather us into His arms with great and multiple mercies. We are to turn away momentarily so we can separate the person from his actions, words, or behavior. Godly anger does not reject the person, it rejects his transgression and with a pure and good conscience seeks a moment of solitude to separate one from the other. I have had numerous examples of God graciously doing this for me.

> *We are to turn away momentarily so we can separate the person from their actions, words, or behavior.*

There are times when His hand is heavy upon me, and I know I am experiencing His displeasure at my behavior. When it becomes more than I can bear, I will repent in earnest and ask for His forgiveness. The heaviness will lift, and I will find my heart filled with His love and promises when I feel so unworthy of them. I know I deserve judgment, yet He bestows mercy instead. He is gathering me back to Himself with His great and gracious mercies. He tells me: "You are still Mine, I still love you, I know you want to do right. I believe you will change. I forgive and I forget it." He wants me to be certain that I am still His child and not rejected by Him even though my actions, words, or behavior are not acceptable to Him.

It's worth noting again: Our first response when angered should be to turn away momentarily, mentally or physically, so we can separate the offense from the offender. The old-fashioned rule of counting to ten is good, but often the time frame is not adequate.

> *I know I deserve judgment, yet He bestows mercy instead.*

Once we have stepped aside from the conflict, then we need to ask, "Why am I so upset?" "What is really going on inside me?" "Do I need to take some time to answer these questions?" This leads us to the second part of the Ephesians verse that began this chapter:

"In your anger do not sin": Do not let the sun go down while you are still angry. (Eph. 4:26 NIV)

The idea of anger being temporary also corresponds to God's admonition "Do not let the sun go down while you are still angry." This is not because of some problem with the dark. All of us have found ourselves upset after the sun has set because we are still awake long after the sun goes down. I believe the sun going down means the end of your day or an appropriate amount of time. When

> ꙮ *Time and anger are intertwined.*

anger exceeds the temporary or transitory stage then it progresses toward the destructive ledge of being angry and sinning. Time and anger are intertwined. The longer an offense goes unresolved, the more deep-seated it becomes. Then the heart becomes a hotbed for a root of bitterness.

In the next chapter we will address the dangers of "bedding down" with our offense.

ꙮ *Heavenly Father,*

I come to you in the name of Jesus. May your Word be a light unto my feet and a lamp unto my path. Show me the pathway of the righteous that I might walk in a manner pleasing in your sight. Teach me to be angry and sin not.

3 Sleeping with the Enemy

When John and I were newlyweds, we seemed to enjoy fighting on quite a regular basis. Most often these verbal matches occurred sometime after dinner but before bed. More often than not after such a heated discourse, I was not ready or willing to wind down and forgive and forget before I went to sleep. (As you may have already guessed, I had a little problem with anger and unforgiveness.) I would punish John with the silent treatment, punctuated by deeply heaved sighs, then plop into bed with my back squarely set against him. I positioned myself so close to the edge of our queen bed, my knees would hang over. I wanted to be certain that no part of my body was in contact with his. After a few minutes of deadly silence and exaggerated repositioning, John would usually say, "Come on, Lisa, let's pray."

"I can pray by myself . . . thank you!" I would huff back without turning.

More silence would follow during which I would feign sleep. Sometimes John would lie there in silence; other times he would leave the room for a little while only to return to do his own huffing and tossing on the bed. Then suddenly John would leap out of bed like a superhero. He would flip on the lights and rip the covers off me.

"We are not going to let the sun go down on our anger!" he would announce authoritatively.

I had been through this on many nights before.

"It's already down! Give me back the covers. I hate it when you do this!" I'd yell as I jumped up to snatch back the comforter.

"No!" John countered. "We have to pray!"

We would enter into a comforter tug-of-war. Finally he would wear me down, and I would pray some halfhearted, hard-hearted prayer, like "I forgive my husband as an act of my will by faith, so he will stop tormenting me and let me go to sleep."

John would wake up happy and rested, and I would wake up tired and grumpy. Then I was mad because he had slept well and I had not.

The reason I had not slept well was because I was still angry. Prayer or no prayer, I did not know how to let go of my anger until I felt the other person had been sufficiently punished or my side of the offense had been adequately voiced and understood. This needed to be followed by the assurance (to my satisfaction) that the misdemeanor would not be repeated. At that time I exacted a kind of penalty, penance, or assurance for the person's offense.

I'm sure you now understand why the short span of time between dinner and bed was insufficient to complete all these proceedings to my satisfaction. So, like a dueling woman of old, I went to bed without satisfaction. A debt was owed and yet to be paid.

Before we both left for work in the morning was not a satisfactory amount of time either. I tended to be totally out of it in the morning. I would glare at my happy husband through sleepy eyes as I stumbled into the shower to be revived. I would later make my way down to breakfast, where I would continue my silent treatment, adding in a few well-placed sighs in case John wasn't noticing my displeasure. Finally he would catch on!

"Honey, is there something wrong?" he would ask.

"Yes," I would answer demurely.

"I thought we settled everything last night," he would counter.

"No, nothing was settled. I just wanted you to stop aggravating me and let me get to sleep," I would lash back. "I've got to get to the store."

I would stomp upstairs with renewed resolve. We would pick up the gauntlet after work. I would have all day to think of my evening arguments.

Inevitably we would come home and run into another disagreement, but this time it would not just include that fight but also the one from the previous night and quite possibly the night before that and the night before that . . . and so on.

> ⤳ *By not resolving my anger with my husband, I put myself in a perpetual state of offense with him.*

By not resolving my anger with my husband, I put myself in a perpetual state of offense with him. I was always either upset or about to become upset.

KNOW WHEN TO LET GO

An integral part of being angry and not sinning is knowing when to let go of your anger. Perpetuating anger perpetuates sin, which perpetuates unforgiveness, which intensifies the anger response. You no longer are dealing with each infraction of displeasure, you are dealing with an accumulation of many infractions against your person. You are repeatedly scraped by the same offense until it is no longer the site of a single injury but a multiple stab wound.

Let's probe deeper into the part of Ephesians 4:26 that says, "Do not let the sun go down on your anger." There is a very important spiritual and physical principle here. When you go to sleep upset, you wake up upset. When you have not extended mercy the night before, it is hard for you to embrace God's mercy in the morning (Ps. 59:16).

In Psalm 4:4, David warned of the danger of inviting anger to sleep with us: "In your anger do not sin; when you are on your beds, search your hearts and be silent" (Ps. 4:4 NIV).

This singing warrior, who possessed a heart that pleased God, shared this wisdom that transcends time and culture. From his experiences he admonished us, "In your anger don't sin; lie down on your beds, search your hearts, and be quiet." Notice David's use of

> ~~❧~~ *When you go to sleep upset, you wake up upset.*

plurals: *beds* and *hearts*. Most of us sleep upon only a single bed just as we each possess only one heart. I believe he understood and was addressing the fact that most anger occurs within relationships. This would encompass couples, family members, and friends. Back then it was not uncommon for married couples to sleep in separate beds. This king is telling his subjects to go to their beds, lie down, wind down, and calmly search their hearts, laying them bare before God.

BE STILL AND KNOW GOD

There is an invitation to revere God, to be still and know. Know what? Know Him as God by allowing Him to reveal Himself in the midst of your pain, conflict, or crisis. He wants to be the final word you hear before sleep overtakes you.

In the quiet stillness say nothing else, don't have the last word. Don't justify your position. Be still and allow God to reveal Himself in the silence. It is a time to gain His insight and perspective and lay down all arguments.

Prayer and meditation before God are often much more about what we hear than what we say. My river of loud and angry words will not wash me clean. They merely express my side, my justifications, my frustrations. No, my wild torrent of reasoning is much too muddy and troubled to cleanse, it only stirs up the bottom and deposits additional debris. It is the still and gentle living fountain from the deep that refreshes and removes the guilt and shame.

DREAMS OF ANGER

But what if you choose to spurn David's counsel and turn to your own reasoning? Your frustration and pain are too real and present to release without sleeping with them at least one night. You embrace anger and draw it close as a shield to your bosom. Though you may drift off to sleep quickly, you most likely will experience a restless or tormented night just as I did because: "As a dream comes when there are many cares, so the speech of a fool when there are many words" (Eccl. 5:3 NIV).

> *Allow God to reveal Himself in the midst of your pain, conflict, or crisis.*

Instead of waking clean, clear, and refreshed, you will find your mind weighed down by all sorts of sordid and angry thoughts. Quite possibly nightmares from the previous night will trail their way into the morning light. Their impressions and experiences will seem strangely real. They can cloak you with a dingy shroud of discouragement or fear. You try to shake them off as dreams, but on these mornings they seem to cling tenaciously.

When we were first married, I frequently woke up angry with John because of some dream I had had the night before. I was convinced that he was an active and willing participant in this bad dream. I was almost certain he knew what he had done and probably would do it again in real life at the earliest opportunity. Of course I was being ridiculous, but it all seemed so real in the dim morning light of my unforgiveness.

Or possibly your night was as void of dreams as it was of rest. You slept, but it was shallow and fitful. Now the remnant of anger from the night before clouds your mind like a dark fog that muddles your thoughts. You forget any apologies or forgiveness and remember only the offense. In the morning light it seems to loom more ominous and offensive. You can't let them off that easy . . . they must pay!

Now you are a victim, and victims don't ask for mercy because they are too busy demanding recompense. You will not embrace God's morning mercy if you awake feeling justified or victimized. If I have learned one thing, it is that I need a lot of mercy, so I have to extend a lot of mercy.

> ✎ *I need a lot of mercy, so I have to extend a lot of mercy.*

Returning to Ephesians we find that God has made even more to say:

"In your anger do not sin": Do not let the sun go down while you are still angry, and do not give the devil a foothold. (Eph. 4:26–27 NIV)

Sinning in your anger by postponing its resolution affords the devil access or a legal entrance into the situation. Matthew Henry's commentary brings out this point: "Let your ears be deaf to whisperers, talebearers, and slanderers." If you are alone and angry in your bed, who else could you possibly hear? Your own thoughts are too loud. They override the still, small voice. No, it is the bolder and louder one you hear. One that keeps excellent and accurate records of previous wrongs committed. The accuser of the brethren dispatches his messengers. They whisper loudly in your ear as you drift off to sleep. They intensify their attack to include talebearing and slander while replaying images of past hurts and pains. Then they project future possibilities of conflict until you wake to find yourself exhausted, angry, and deeply offended.

Don't forget how the Bible describes the devil: "Be self-controlled and alert. Your enemy the devil prowls around like a roaring lion looking for someone to devour" (1 Peter 5:8 NIV).

He is prowling and watching for those who are not self-controlled and alert. Another translation warns us to be sober and vigilant. The opposite of sober is drunk. A drunk is often unaware of what is really going on around him. His perceptions and perspectives are blurred. His response time is slowed and his reasoning distorted. To be vigilant is to be watchful and on guard; it implies to stay awake and attentive.

Lions often hunt at night. The devil is compared to a roaring lion on the lookout for someone to devour. He obviously does not literally come into our rooms and physically consume us. If that were the case, each of us would be certain to resolve any anger issues before allowing our head to hit the pillow. No, he consumes us in other, subtler ways. Though they are less obvious, they are no less of a danger to us. He consumes our joy, our peace, our rest, our strength, as well as our health, our relationships, and our thoughts. He replaces the peaceful silence with a din of accusations. The quiet, reverential fear of the Lord is overshadowed by tormenting and torturous fear. I believe God used the terror and persistence of a hungry lion to visually illustrate the determination and persistence of Satan's pursuit. He catches the scent of offense and unresolved anger as a lion detects the blood of his prey.

> *The devil is compared to a roaring lion on the lookout for someone to devour.*

SLEEP IN THE LIGHT

Perhaps on this earth we will never have full comprehension of just how important it is to obey the warnings of God. Those with a childlike obedience who don't offer lengthy explanations are often granted greater spiritual authority than the learned who choose to lean on their own understanding. Obedience protects, but the wisdom of man is foolishness to God. In comparison to His, our wisdom is merely folly.

I live in Colorado, and if a ranger came to my front door and informed me that there was a wild and ravenous bear on the loose in our neighborhood I would not only take heed, I would also ask him if he could suggest any helpful precautions. If he said, "It is important that you go to sleep tonight with your lights on," I would, even though I prefer to sleep in the dark. I would continue to sleep with the lights on until the bear was captured or killed.

God wants us to sleep in the light of His truth, whether we fully understand why or not. If we are warned so succinctly to be sober, vigilant, alert, and self-controlled, we would be wise to heed the warning.

I have learned this lesson the hard way. I thought I was wiser and that I could manage going to sleep angry. It didn't begin in my marriage but early on as a child and young adult. I would lie in bed and meditate on my anger or the offense. I envisioned revenge and my idea of justice. I was not a Christian, so I never considered God's wisdom or insights during my bitter meditations. I allowed the reasoning of this world to dictate my attitudes and responses.

> The wisdom of man is foolishness to God.

Studies have proven that most of us develop our anger response as small children. Patterns are established through positive or negative reinforcement. We learned what worked or got us attention, and we repeated it so often it became a habit.

Some of you may have made the dangerous decision to go to bed angry in ignorance as I did as a child. Others of you may have known the truth yet chose your own wisdom. Still others of you don't go to your bed angry at another individual. No, your anger is leveled at yourself. You go to sleep disappointed and upset with yourself and imagine by punishing yourself throughout the night you will awake changed and different. But this is not true. The nightly punishment will not be constructive but destructive.

You are mistaken to think anger is only destructive when vented on others. When I wasn't upset with my husband, I often was disappointed with myself. I would go to bed each night and recite a mental list of each and every failing from the day. I would beat myself up with it, whipping myself with the shame of any remembered mistake in an attempt to pay a penance for my infractions.

> ◈ *Patterns are established through positive or negative reinforcement.*

I am not saying that it is wrong to look back over your day and realize you have made mistakes or to wish you had done things differently. It is healthy to allow the Holy Spirit to bring to your remembrance any grievous word or deed. But this is best accomplished in the stillness of your bed as you read your Bible or commune with the Lord in your heart. What I did, and what I am afraid many of you may do, was to berate myself in the night and then allow the weight of it to smother me as I slept. In the morning I would allow myself to pray and ask forgiveness, but by then guilt had such a stranglehold on me it was difficult to believe His mercy was new every morning.

For example, if I was disappointed with the way I had handled my children during the day, I pressed the issue very heavily: *I should be more patient.* Then I would allow guilt to weigh on me until I felt hopelessly horrible, and in this despair and self-loathing I would go to sleep. My hope was to wake up feeling so bad about my impatience that it would not be replayed. Instead I would wake up feeling hopeless and like a failure. This would weigh me down and make

> ◈ *Guilt is darkness; mercy is light.*

me feel overwhelmed, which made the challenges of the day seem that much more taxing. I had set myself up to fail again. I have learned both self-loathing and anger are destructive. Inflicting guilt does not reform our relationships with others, nor will it work on you.

Jesus understood that the guilt from our sins and failings was too much for us to bear, so He bore it for us. He wants our faults to be exposed by the light of His truth, which is His Word. This light heals what it reveals. As we draw closer to Him, He dispels the darkness of our lives until it becomes light. Guilt is darkness; mercy is light. The following is one of my favorite verses. It paints a beautiful image of the process of transformation.

> But the path of the just is as the shining light, that shineth more and more unto the perfect day. The way of the wicked is as darkness: they know not at what they stumble. (Prov. 4:18–19 KJV)

In a later chapter we will cover the important issue of forgiving yourself. But for now you need to realize you are on the path of the just. Though you are not perfect, you are walking toward the perfect day. Now is the time to allow your heart to be purged. Won't you embrace God's Word and wisdom? If so, pray with me.

✎ *Dear Heavenly Father,*

I come to You in the name of Jesus. I have been guilty of sleeping with the enemy. Forgive me. I no longer will sleep with rage, guilt, or anger. I will no longer allow darkness to shroud my heart. I want the light of Your Word and love to permeate my heart with truth. I will be still and quiet on my bed as I seek Your counsel. I embrace the promise of Your Word: "When you lie down, you will not be afraid; when you lie down, your sleep will be sweet" (Prov. 3:24 NIV). I humble myself in obedience under Your mighty hand. I resist the devil, and he must flee from the areas where I have granted him a foothold. Cover me as I rest, for "I will lie down and sleep in peace, for you alone, O LORD, make me dwell in safety" (Ps. 4:8 NIV).

4 Ready . . . Aim . . . Fire

These visually charged words help illustrate the fallen anger cycle—the progression from anger to sin. After hearing, "Ready, aim, fire," you can't help but envision them. We can see someone who is perhaps relaxed or unprepared snap to attention and into the ready position. Posture becomes erect and their hands hover over their weapon of defense. Next we see them lift the weapon and look intently for their target, sighting it for accuracy, mentally noting the victim's distance and readiness. Once aim is accomplished, all that remains is the decision to fire and the simple act of squeezing the trigger or releasing an arrow. Finally there is a pause as we watch for the target's response.

I feel this sequence of words accurately and vividly portrays not only the act of firing but also the progression from anger to sin or, to be more precise, the progression from anger to rage to fury.

A State of Readiness

In Neil Clark Warren's book, *Make Anger Your Ally*, anger is described as "completely natural, perfectly legitimate. It is that internal happening which prepares us to cope with hurtful, frustrating, and fearful experiences." And "anger is simply a state of physical readiness." He goes on to explain, "When we are angry, we are prepared to act." Anger in its

23

purest form is the physical ability or readiness to respond. Of course, there is nothing wrong with being ready, willing, and able to respond, or should we say to shoot. No harm has yet been done, we are just booting up for what might lie ahead. The gun has not been raised; we are merely aware of a heightened sense of the possible need for them.

Ready is when adrenaline begins to course through our veins, transporting blood to our muscles as they tense in response. Even our breathing steps up to meet any possible increase in demand for air, and the drum of our heart increases the tempo. We are in a state of excited irritation. Those around us may not even be aware of our heightened sense of readiness. They did not hear our inner drill sergeant's command of *"Ready!"* even though it resounded off every nerve cell in our body.

There is an enemy out there! Be on your guard! Brace yourself to attack or be attacked! Even now you gauge your response by the intensity of your feelings. How upset am I? How reasonable am I? Or has my reasoning been overridden? The emotional and physical forces of anger have prepared us for something, and we're ready, but now what? Do we hit or run?

Suddenly, the second command is issued, "Aim!" We realize by doing this we will make the weapon known. If any were wondering if we were upset . . . they know now. We lift and level the weapon of choice at our target. We have taken aim, but how far will we go? Perhaps just the mere identification of the offender will alleviate the need for further action. We are now prepared for confrontation. We are armed but possibly still not dangerous. Merely aiming doesn't necessarily come with a commitment to shoot. Whether a gun is fired or not, once it is aimed at another person, all the immediate dynamics of the relationship change.

Rage continues to progress to fury as our temperature rises, and at this point we are committed to shoot. An element of desperation and fear has been introduced. We must destroy or be destroyed, so we sight the offending human or humans as targets and draw a bead on them. But where do we hit them? Do we want to temporarily wound them, or perhaps cripple them, so they will walk with a limp hereafter? Or will it be necessary to eliminate them completely from the picture? In that case we must go for a vital organ such as the heart. In our agitated state can we safely make such a vital decision? We must! There is an urgency pushing us onward. We now feel certain that it must be the head or the heart we attack. We carefully and deliberately take aim and wait for the next signal—"Fire!"

We squeeze the trigger, recoiling from the force we have discharged. For a moment we close our eyes to blink away the image that awaits us, only to open them immediately.

There before us is bleeding destruction. It is so much more real and horrible than we imagined possible. We are shocked by the devastation and begin to question the commands of the drill sergeant, who is now oddly silent.

What have we witnessed? We watched as the natural response of "anger" was escalated to the dangerous final and regrettable stage of fury. This example illustrates the dividing line between constructive anger and destructive fury. Anger would be the emotional and physical preparedness, rage would be the introduction of the weapon, and fury would be the unrestrained decision to use it for destruction.

WEAPONS OF ANGER

Too often we have lived the ready, aim, fire scenario without the involvement of physical weapons. Our weapons are less tangible and come in the form of words, thoughts, or actions. Perhaps even now your mind is wandering back to a time when a gun of this sort went off in your hand. Some of you remember looking up only to discover someone else had you in *their* sights. It is important we go into some detailed and practical examples of rage and fury because so *often much of what we call anger is not really anger at all but the progressive stages of rage or fury.*

25

Remember the story in the first chapter of when I threw the plate? While I was washing dishes, my emotional tension brought me into the ready stage of anger. I knew I was agitated and was struggling to keep myself in check. Then it hit me. I allowed a word or phrase used by my husband to push me beyond anger and into the realm of rage. I identified a target in my husband. At that point I still could have restrained myself, but I chose to allow rage and fury to reign, and I released the full force of my emotions as I threw the plate.

> ~~~ *Our weapons come in the form of words, thoughts, or actions.*

Now let's look at a scriptural example of ready, aim, and fire. It is the familiar account of Cain and his brother Abel. Even though you are familiar with this passage, please take the time to review it as though it were the first time you read it.

> In the course of time Cain brought some of the fruits of the soil as an offering to the Lord. But Abel brought fat portions from some of the firstborn of his flock. The Lord looked with favor on Abel and his offering, but on Cain and his offering he did not look with favor. (Gen. 4:3–5 NIV)

Oh no! There is a problem. God bestowed His favor on both Abel and his offering but withheld His favor from Cain and his offering. Imagine the emotional intensity of this. Cain had fully expected his labor to be rewarded by the Holy One. Perhaps he even felt his offering was superior to Abel's. After all, he had labored for a long period and Abel had merely slaughtered sheep in a single day. Cain was shocked by the revelation. He knew God was God and did not want to admit the possibility that he himself might have messed up . . . it must be Abel's fault. Somehow Abel had displaced the blessing from Cain's life. Cain was upset, very upset. He was more than ready.

WHY?

> So Cain was very angry, and his face was downcast. Then the LORD said to Cain, "Why are you angry? Why is your face downcast? If you do what is right, will you not be accepted? But if you do not do what is right, sin is crouching at your door; it desires to have you, but you must master it." (Gen. 4:5–7 NIV)

God will ask us the same questions: *Why? What is it that has you so emotionally charged at the moment? What is the real issue?*

God was aware of Cain's anger and asked him a very important question, "Why?" God already knew why he was upset; He wanted Cain to know. If Cain had taken the time to honestly answer this question, the following tragedy could have been averted. But Cain never dealt with the real issue of *why* he was upset. *It is always easier to turn on another than to face the truth.* When Cain did not answer, God reached out and spoke to him at the level of truth where the real issue was. He reminded an offended Cain, "If you do what is right, will you not be accepted?" He assured Cain that doing right would bring acceptance and then warned, "But if you do not do what is right, sin is crouching at your door; it desires to have you, but you must master it."

Cain was in the ready position. He was angry, and although he had yet to take aim, he was thinking about it. God knew this and strongly warned him the choice was his to master sin or, should I say, harness his building rage. Cain did not and instead waited for an opportunity to execute his vengeance. He had Abel in his sights, and all that remained was the opportune time.

> Now Cain said to his brother Abel, "Let's go out to the field." And while they were in the field, Cain attacked his brother Abel and killed him. (Gen. 4:8 NIV)

Perhaps he lured Abel out to the field by asking for his help or by inviting him to look at the remainder of his harvest. But all along Cain's purpose was to kill Abel. He had not heeded God's warning but had given himself over to sin, allowing it to master him.

Then the LORD said to Cain, "Where is your brother Abel?" "I don't know," he replied. "Am I my brother's keeper?" The LORD said, "What have you done? Listen! Your brother's blood cries out to me from the ground." (Gen. 4:9–10 NIV)

Cain knew exactly where his brother was . . . he was dead and buried in the field, surrounded by the fruit of the offering God had rejected. Isn't it interesting that Cain knew how to sacrifice, but he reserved this for his brother rather than as an act of obedience? We can assume both brothers had learned about the sacrifice of a spotless lamb from their parents, Adam and Eve. Yet Cain had allowed his anger to run the course of destruction from rage to fury and wrath.

If we do right we will be accepted, and we still have the ability to master sin. Though most of us have never literally murdered our brother, many of us have witnessed the devastation of careless words, actions, and premeditated slander and gossip. To successfully deal with anger we must always first honestly answer the question God asked of Cain, "Why are you angry?"

≈≈≈ Heavenly Father,

I come to You clothed in the righteousness of Jesus. Lord, I want truth in my innermost being. I ask that You open the eyes of my heart so I might know why I am angry. Search my heart, reveal to me day by day when my reaction to something is anger so I can ask myself why.

5 Crimes of Passion

It was an idyllic morning. My dear friend Chris had stopped by with her children, and we had enjoyed a few stolen moments together sipping flavored coffee sweetened with ice cream on my back screened-in porch. We watched contentedly as our four children played together happily in the backyard. There had not been one squabble between my two kids and her two children. The sun danced on their little heads as they darted between trees and scaled the swing set. There was a gentle breeze pushing away the Florida humidity, and the phone had not rung once. We had enjoyed uninterrupted conversation for nearly an hour! In the peacefulness of it all, it would have been easy to forget the many things we both had yet to accomplish. We sighed, knowing it couldn't last. Our coffee was gone and soon it would be time for lunch. As we called our little ones in I smugly reflected on my children, "What happy, well-adjusted children I have!" I patted their heads as they scrabbled through the open French door. Such great behavior should be awarded all around . . . they had all shared so well and played so lovingly.

"Wait a minute, Chris. We will walk you out. I have something I want to give the kids since they all played so well together." I slipped into the kitchen and grabbed a bag of gummy dinosaurs.

"Here is a special treat for after lunch. Each of you may pick two. Austin, you can pass them out."

29

I poured a generous amount into the hand of my curly-headed two-year-old. He extended his hand somewhat hesitantly to his six-year-old friend, who gingerly chose two of the brightly colored gummies. Next, Addison, my four-year-old, took two. My friend's daughter was reaching for her two when suddenly Austin's hand closed in a tight fist.

"Austin, give Richie her dinosaurs," I encouraged.

"No," Austin replied. As he glanced up I recognized the determination in his eyes.

"Austin, there are a lot more inside. Give her two, and if you don't like the ones that are left, you can choose from the ones in the bag."

His only response was to wrap himself around the mailbox post and shake his head no.

Now I was getting embarrassed. I had been reasonable and even recognized now that he had not been the best choice to distribute candy, but he was not budging. My friend really needed to go, so I ran in and got the remainder of the bag of candy and offered it to her daughter. As they climbed into car seats and seat belts, Austin remained firmly attached to the mailbox.

I decided to ignore him for the moment and said my good-byes and apologized for Austin's rudeness. As I waved them out of sight I called to him. "Come on, Austin, we're going in now." Addison happily ran in, but Austin refused to leave his post. I nonchalantly walked toward the mailbox, hoping none of my neighbors were witnessing the episode. When I realized he could not be persuaded to come in, I glanced both ways and peeled him off the mailbox. Of course a car drove by at that moment. I tried to look casual as I dragged a kicking, screaming two-year-old across the front lawn. *What if someone thought I was kidnapping him!*

Gone were the prideful thoughts of my self-righteous parenting.

Once inside things did not get better. I opened his fist, removed the sweaty, mutilated gummies, and told him to go up to his bedroom until he had calmed down. I then went into the kitchen. But he had no intention of calming down or of going to his room.

"I'm not going to my room!" he declared.

"Yes, you are," I countered calmly, remaining in the kitchen.

"I'm not going to my room!" he yelled louder.

"Sure you are. You are going to obey me." I kept my voice calm and quiet.

"No! I'm not going to my room!" he yelled.

But this time I noticed his voice was no longer coming from the foyer but from halfway up the stairs.

"Yes, you will," I replied.

I motioned to Addison to quietly peek around the corner and tell me where Austin was.

"He is sitting at the top of the stairs," Addison reported with a whisper.

"I'm not going in my room!" Austin yelled again. This time I just ignored his threats and began to carry on a conversation with Addison. Austin continued his declarations of independence for another fifteen minutes or so but with less and less zeal. Then I heard him say emphatically, "I'm not going to sleep. I'm not going to take a nap!"

He repeated this phrase a few more times, then there was silence. I peeked around the corner, expecting to find him asleep at the top of the stairs, but he was nowhere in sight. I quietly slipped upstairs and found him sound asleep on his bed.

WHY DO WE FIGHT SO HARD?

At some level Austin knew he was wrong and even knew what he needed. He had put himself down for a nap, protesting all the way. Why had he fought so hard? He was obviously exhausted and tired.

In answer, Why do *we* fight so hard? Especially when we are exhausted and tired. I believe it is often for the same reason my son fought.

In his mind there was definitely a reason for his protest. Right or wrong, he felt his person had been violated. He did not want to share the dinosaurs. As he watched the pile of them diminish in his hand, something in him snapped. He closed his fist, signaling enough was enough. *I don't care what my mommy or anyone else says, I am not sharing any more of these.* When he awoke from his nap in a reasonable and calm state, I let him know that his behavior was inappropriate and would not be rewarded. After all, he didn't even get a gummy dinosaur out of it.

> ✒ *Often children exemplify in a raw and obvious way what adults have learned to gloss over with niceties.*

Mind you, I am not defending his behavior or his selfishness. Often children exemplify in a raw and obvious way what adults have learned to gloss over with niceties. Our polite contempt often clouds the issue.

I had stayed calm during this encounter, not because I am so adept at motherhood (Are any of us really? I daily need God's grace and wisdom in the arena of child rearing), but because I recognized myself in him. I had often struggled with feeling frustrated and violated without knowing how to put it into words. So I made unreasonable declarations of independence as if to say, "I will do this but only under protest, and it will be when I am ready . . . It is going to be my timing and idea." We will always become angry when we feel violated, when some part of our person is actually or perceived to be trespassed.

> ✒ *People become upset regarding areas in which they feel great passion.*

We already have defined anger as an aroused or agitated physical state of heightened awareness; therefore, we do not have to step too far to realize that anger also encompasses passion. People become upset regarding areas in which they feel great passion.

For example, there are certain areas you can cross me in and I will not be upset or ruffled by the violation. These areas have varied and shifted as I have hopefully matured and my life settings and frames of reference have changed.

The Passion of Anger

When I was in high school there was nothing I was more passionate about or terrified by than the prospect of being made fun of because of my artificial eye. I remember one incident in particular where I reacted in an outburst of rage. It was a home football game, and a number of friends and myself were squeezing through the bleachers to get to our seats. I always hated this because I was aware I was in everyone's way and I was extremely self-conscious. I was the last person in the procession to the seats, and as I scooted by the annoyed spectators I apologized. As I passed one particularly rough, big guy he said, "That's okay . . . one eye." Immediately my face flushed. I stopped and turned back toward him. "What did you call me?" I questioned him, daring him to say it to my face instead of my back side. He met my gaze and said again, "One eye." Before I knew what had happened my entire Coke was in his face. I turned and looked for my friends, but they were already seated and lost in the sea of high schoolers. I made my way through a shocked crowd, shaking with anger and fear. I did not even remember what he said in response. Of course, the entire section of people had seen my outburst yet none of them had heard his words. I found my friends and sat down. Soon I received word that this boy intended to beat me up after the game. I was too angry to care. I sent back some ignorant remark, like "I don't care. He doesn't scare me!" But it was a lie, I was terrified. I clung to my friends until I was safely in my parents' car and dreaded returning to school the following week. I was certain he would find me and kill me one way or another. Surprisingly enough he never bothered me again, but I lived under the constant fear that someone else would call me any of the assorted names they had for me . . . and they did.

I was impassioned when it came to my eye. When someone called me Cyclops my world came spinning to an end. I longed to leave school and hide in my room. But that was more than twenty years ago. Now I am married and feel secure and loved in my relationships with my husband and friends. I have learned that my looks are not the measure of my person (Thank God!). My horizons have been greatly expanded since high school. I am no longer defined by or limited to my high school experiences. I became a Christian and learned to look beyond myself.

I am a grown adult now with four children of my own. I don't care who calls me names, but I don't do well when people mess with my children. They are my new passion. My initial response is to immediately jump in and protect them from the possibility of pain. The anger at their treatment does not trigger a reoccurrence of my personal pain but rather a passionate, protective response somewhere between that of a mother bear and a normal parent. I am aware that I am possibly excessively passionate in this area, so I try to always step back and see if my protection is really necessary. After all, I have four sons, and they don't rattle quite as easily as I did.

Let's look back at my bleacher incident. At the time I would have thought it was impossible *not* to throw the Coke. I couldn't imagine overlooking or choosing to ignore the comment. To me it was a life-and-death issue. Had the young man actually attacked me, I would have fought with all my might and never dreamed of apologizing for throwing a Coke in his face. I was an ignorant, passionate heathen! But where is my passion today? Is it because I lack passion that I would no longer react to the same event? No, I still have passion, but it is no longer important to me. It is no longer a violation. Yet this does not mean I do not value opinions in other areas of my life, and it is quite possible these areas will again change with the passage of another twenty years.

Let's further expand our working definition of anger. *It is a heightened physical and emotional state of preparedness to defend something about which we are passionate, and we are passionate when something is important to us.* We usually are not angered by the trivial unless it ties into something on a grander scale that is important to us.

Now let's look at passion. Too frequently our culture limits passion to the confines of the sexual, but passion encompasses a much broader spectrum and is evident in an individual long before sexual desire is awakened. We need a clearer definition of *passion*. Its definition is unique because it embraces both extremes of human emotion: love and hate. Passion is closely associated with the following words of attachment: *emotion, enthusiasm, excitement, desire, fondness, love, affection, infatuation, craving,* and *lust.* It is also associated with these equally strong words of alienation and estrangement: *fire, outburst, fury, ire, anger, indignation, rage, resentment, vehemence,* and *wrath.*

Bearing in mind the above meanings of *passion,* let's examine a verse from the book of James:

Blessed is the man who endures temptation; for when he has been proved, he will receive the crown of life which the Lord has promised to those who love Him. (1:12 NKJV)

This is the promise and admonishment that precede the warning. I believe this goes right along with the warning Cain received. It is the promise of blessing to those who choose the path of life. Of course, Cain did not endure or master the temptation but instead murdered his brother. The Scripture goes on to say,

35

Let no one say when he is tempted, "I am tempted by God"; for God cannot be tempted by evil, nor does He Himself tempt anyone. But each one is tempted when he is drawn away by his own desires and enticed. (1:13–14 NKJV)

EXCUSES, EXCUSES

Allow *no one* to say that God is causing him or her to be tempted. I believe another way of saying this would be, Don't even try to blame it on God. Maybe you remember Flip Wilson's character Geraldine, who always made the excuse, "The devil made me do it!" I don't actually think believers would ever say, "God made me do it! He made me commit adultery" or "He made me shoot that man." I believe there is another way that we inadvertently blame God. It is when we say, "I couldn't help it" or "I just couldn't control myself." It is when we contradict God, who says we can do all things through Christ who strengthens us, by saying sin desires us and we are not able to master it. We may not say it with our mouths but more than likely we will say it with our lifestyles.

> ✒ *Allow no one to say that God is causing him or her to be tempted.*

DON'T DWELL ON IT

Then, when desire has conceived, it gives birth to sin; and sin, when it is full-grown, brings forth death. (1:15 NKJV)

When desire or passions are allowed to go unchecked in our thought life, they leave the womb of the hidden and silent and come forth into the tangible and present as sin. An obvious example of this would be a man and woman who sexually desire one another. They visit images of the object of their desire often in their thought lives; long before there has been any physical contact there is extensive mental fantasizing. It progresses from a passing thought in the day that at first may even seem a violation (*What made me think about him that way?*), then progresses into a meditation in the night (*I wonder what it would be like to be with him to share his attention and affection?*). Soon the line between fantasy and reality is blurred. Thinking about each other turns toward longing. At first it is an emotional pull, then it becomes a physical one. Fantasizing alone is no longer enough . . . there must be contact (*Does he feel the same way? I must know!*). Perhaps this contact appears innocent, merely a testing of the waters, but it quickly moves forward. The flames of desire have been fanned by the meditations of this desirous individual, and now it is raging out of control and threatening to burn them if it is not satiated. Physical contact follows, and it is so intense they are swept away in a passionate flood and fire of their own making. Adultery or fornication follows, and ultimately it brings death. Death to marriages lost to divorce, death to freedom as they become slaves to passion, death to sexual purity as marriage beds are defiled.

But the same is true with anger. Someone offends you, and at first you only think about the offense occasionally. You entertain what you would really like to say to them if you were ever given the chance. You think of other people who might need to hear about their offense against you. Possibly they could advise you. If this is someone you've had a relationship with for a while, you might replay former infractions you have stored in your memory banks. Now the offense has grown and needs more of your thought life. It demands to be noticed, and the next time you see this individual you find that you are uncomfortable with them. You avoid looking them in the eye and either feel a false sense of superiority or a distasteful distancing from them. In this case the passion we speak of is resentment. Growing in the womb of your mind is an offense. It is not long before you find yourself becoming short and impatient with this person. You are upset when you even hear them praised by another.

FROM ANGER TO RESENTMENT TO . . .

The sin begins. Anger has moved from temporary displeasure to enduring resentment. It has progressed from anger to rage, and rage always seeks a form of release.

> ~ *Rage seeks punishment or vengeance at all cost.*

It is too uncomfortable to hold within for very long. You lash out in rage, you gossip and slander in an effort to punish them. Rage seeks punishment or vengeance at all cost. Hatred creeps in, and death soon follows in broken relationships, destroyed trust, and deep roots of bitterness. Death always represents the absence of life. Hate blackens the heart by blotting out life.

Whoever hates his brother is a murderer, and you know that no murderer has eternal life abiding in him. (1 John 3:15 NKJV)

Let's look at this Scripture. First of all, it says *whoever*. This includes every one. There is no exception clause footnoted at the bottom of the page that reads, "This excludes everyone who has *really* been mistreated by their brother or brethren." When the Scripture reads *whoever, anyone*, or *everyone*, it means that it applies to each of us personally. We don't have the option of saying, But you don't understand what they did! When God gives an all-inclusive instruction like this, it is not only a truth He wants us to submit to but also one for which He will equip us to live out. God said that whoever hates his brother is a murderer. That is strong. I don't want to be called a murderer. Yet I can honestly say there have been times in my Christian walk when I have found hatred in the dark recesses of my heart. Does this mean I am eternally condemned as an eternal outlaw or even a murderer? Yes, if I allow it to remain and grow unchecked; no, if I do not.

Each of us has experienced the empowering grace and the covering mercy of God. No sin is too dark or heinous that He will not forgive it. Doesn't God forgive murderers? Then why does God say a murderer has no eternal life abiding in him? First, there is a vast difference between someone who commits the physical act of murder, whether as a crime of passion or a premeditated crime, only later to repent of his crime, and one who lives with a perpetual state of homicide in his heart.

We must view this from a kingdom perspective, not from the perspective of our earthly judicial system. When a citizen

> *We are not governed by the laws of this earth but by the ways of heaven.*

of this earth murders another, he may very well serve a life sentence as a payment of sorts for his crime. But we are no longer mere citizens of this earth, for Scripture tells us, "Now, therefore, you are no longer strangers and foreigners, but fellow citizens with the saints and members of the household of God" (Eph. 2:19 NKJV).

We are not governed by the laws of this earth but by the ways of heaven. Heaven does not govern by outward rules and regulations etched in stone, but by the secret code written on our hearts. Dead, lifeless rules etched in stone are for dead, hard hearts. The law of liberty is not for hearts of stone but for those of flesh. First John 3:15 was written to Christians as a warning that when we hate our brother, eternal life no longer resides within us. In the kingdom of earth you must physically kill to be labeled a murderer, but in the kingdom or household of God, all you have to do is hate.

It is important to note that hearts of flesh have a greater capacity for both love and pain than stony hearts do. If hatred is allowed because of an intense hurt or pain, it will slowly but surely displace the eternal life and forgiveness of God in our life. We find ourselves heavy and drained. We will find it harder and harder to forgive others, even those who have not previously offended us. Anger is no longer passing and temporary, it becomes our passion. It is exhausting to live constantly on the edge of rage. At first our hearts convict us in an attempt to bring to light our true condition, then they begin to condemn us as that light is replaced by reasoning and rage.

> _It is exhausting to live constantly on the edge of rage._

But even the hardened hearts of Christians can be liberated by the hammering truth of God's Word. I already confessed that I have found hate in my heart since becoming a Christian. Am I forever condemned? No, I choose not to allow it to remain. You must guard your heart, zealously assuring that it remains free from unresolved offenses that have been encouraged by allowing anger to progress to the state of rage, fury, or wrath.

For some of you the message in this book is just such a hammer. You may even now be fighting a reasoning war in your mind. One voice brings up the faces and names of those who have hurt you and begs you to forgive and release, while another voice continues to justify any hatred or resentment of others. Surrender to the first voice. Stop justifying your rage and allow the Holy Spirit to walk closer with you on the path of life.

> _Heavenly Father,_
>
> _I come to You in the name of Jesus. I confess there is hidden hatred in my heart. Lord, I don't want it to reside there any longer. I choose life, not death; blessing, not cursing. I renounce hatred and repent of it with the same intensity I would of murder. Thank You for opening the eyes of my heart and revealing truth. Teach me to be angry without sinning._

6 When It Hurts Too Bad

It is not unlikely that you might be thinking, *You don't understand my pain. You don't know what was done to me. You don't know how badly I hurt.* You are right, I do not—but there is Someone who does. Maybe you were molested or abused by someone you once trusted. Maybe you were raped or violated by a stranger. Possibly you were abandoned and left alone by someone who promised to always be there. Perhaps your child died a violent or senseless death. Someone you love was mistreated. Your parents disappointed or rejected you. You never felt good enough. You were mocked for the color of your skin. You were made fun of for a handicap. Or you were betrayed by a friend.

THE ROOTS OF BITTERNESS

Any one of these tragedies is painful enough to carry with it seeds to a root of bitterness. It is a wretched trick of Satan to plant his dark seeds into the soil of our wounded hearts, but he does. I believe it is quite possibly when we are the most vulnerable that he slips in. He encourages us to remember the pain, to hold it in and not to release it. He lies while he promises us that if we will hold in the pain and allow it to permanently impress its memory upon our hearts, it will somehow protect us from future violations. He encourages us not to release our anger at the end of the day, but to draw strength from it by perpetuating its influence in our lives. Again, this is a lie.

Broken hearts are like broken ground—both are good for the sowing of seed. God longs for us to heed His warning, draw near to Him in our pain, and allow the Holy Spirit to plant seeds of comfort from His Word into the wounds of our hearts. These seeds may grow slowly, but they heal and bring forth life. When first planted you may find yourself feeling weak and vulnerable, but these seeds grow in secret, healing us from the inside out.

> ✒ *It is a wretched trick of Satan to plant his dark seeds into the soil of our wounded hearts.*

Satan also longs to plant seeds. He searches like a ravenous lion drawn by the scent of a wound. He lulls us into sleeping with our anger and plants the tares of bitterness while we wrestle in our sleep. We awake with a trickle of vengeance in our veins. Initially it is like caffeine, supplying a boost to a weary soul. The effect is temporary, and just as caffeine depletes our body of healthful necessary nutrients to accomplish its goal, so the root of bitterness chokes the nourishing seedlings of the Word of God.

Weeds always grow faster and easier than plants do. They are wild plants that travel freely, adapting to any type of soil they find. On the other hand, the life-giving seeds of fruits or vegetables must be cultivated carefully and are easily choked out by surrounding weeds or the wrong soil conditions.

> Looking carefully lest anyone fall short of the grace of God; lest any root of bitterness springing up cause trouble, and by this many become defiled. (Heb 12:15 NKJV)

To look carefully is to keep diligent and consistent watch over. We are warned in this verse that carelessness in this area may cause us to fall short of the grace of God. This gives rise to a root of bitterness. The description makes me think of times as a young girl when I was given the task of pulling weeds. I was always in a hurry to get the job done and over with so I could play. In my carelessness I would often snap off the top of the weed instead of pulling it up by the root. It would not have been too difficult to pull up the weed root and all, but that meant a little more effort. I had to pierce the dirt to grab hold of the base, and I didn't want to mess with that. Surely with the stem and all the leaves gone that plant would not survive, and my mother would never know what was underground. I would rake dirt over the gnarled stumps and run along. A few weeks later another weed would be in its place. Often it was smaller than the original one I had snapped off, but it now possessed an amazingly stubborn root system. My mother showed me how it would now be necessary for me to dig around the base of the plant and expose enough of the root to get a death grip on it. What would normally be an easy chore had now turned into a tedious battle.

The root of bitterness chokes the nourishing seedlings of the Word of God.

How often do we do the same thing with the gardens of our hearts? We are careless when it comes to weeding, and instead of uprooting weeds of wrong thinking we merely snap them off at the visual level and hope no one will see the root lying beneath the surface. We fail to allow the Holy Spirit to do a deep work. We do not receive the words that pierce and penetrate; we want the ones that will smooth things over. On the surface we look weeded, but just under it we harbor all sorts of unresolved issues. The flowers in the bed begin to fade and wither, but still we persist. Then suddenly the root of bitterness springs up. While it was underground it had entwined itself into the root system of viable healthy plants and drained them.

We dig around this bitter root, amazed at the depth and reach of it. We put on gloves so we can grip it and pull with all our might, always careful to walk our hands ever closer to its base to avoid once again breaking it and leaving another root remnant in the soil. As it comes up it displaces many flowers, and we are left with a mess that all can see!

HOW DOES A ROOT OF BITTERNESS DEFILE US?

Bitter roots cause trouble, and they defile. Something that once was pure is contaminated, tainted, adulterated, and corrupted. Our tender hearts, carefully planted with good seed, are permeated by tenacious roots of destructive and bitter poison. This is the reason we are warned: "Above all else, guard your heart, for it is the wellspring of life" (Prov. 4:23 NIV).

Weeds will drain and pollute your supply of living water. The root comes out, and you feel empty and lifeless. You can live for a while without food but not very long without water. "Above all else" means

> ✎ *Bitter roots cause trouble, and they defile.*

it is of utmost importance that our hearts be guarded. You place armor where you are the most vulnerable. You lock in safes what you value most. Your heart is your source of life or death, the very chamber of your soul. It should be kept under lock and key. A guard should be stationed at every possible entryway.

How does a root of bitterness defile us? In Acts 8:23, Peter rebuked Simon the sorcerer: "For I see that you are full of bitterness and captive to sin" (NIV). Simon had believed and was baptized, yet there remained weeds in his heart. This caused him to irreverently attempt to purchase the free gift of the Holy Spirit so that those he laid hands on could receive the Spirit. Bitterness holds us captive to sin. Because of unresolved offenses we will attempt to use the precious things of God to validate ourselves rather than to equip others. We will inadvertently mix the precious with the vile. The pure and precious may enter our heart, but it soon is defiled and polluted by the root of bitterness that resides therein. The grace of God is twisted into a license to sin instead of an empowerment to walk in obedience.

Ridding Yourself of Bitterness

In the book of Ephesians, Paul admonished us to

> Get rid of all bitterness, rage and anger, brawling and slander, along with every form of malice. Be kind and compassionate to one another, forgiving each other, just as in Christ God forgave you. (4:31–32 NIV)

Paul described this in Colossians as the removing of the old garment of self and putting on the new self, which is being renewed in the image of the Creator. It is an exchange of citizenship from the kingdom of darkness into the kingdom of light. Where unhealthy expressions or cycles of anger may at one time have *appeared* to protect us, we now see they actually defiled and enslaved us.

Roots of bitterness will spring up at the most inopportune times, when they are the most inconvenient to be dealt with. Though they may be inconvenient, they will become deadly if ignored. Don't be tricked into allowing them to remain unchecked, and never snap off the visible part thinking it will deter the root. It will not; it will only serve to strengthen it. Too often we are satisfied with the mere illusion that everything is under control and all right when actually there is a storm of dangerous proportions raging just under the smooth surface.

Ephesians ties bitterness, rage, anger, and every form of malice to unforgiveness. The secret to ridding yourself of a root of bitterness is to forgive and release those who have deeply wounded you. I am not saying it will be easy to do, but I am saying there will be enduring hardship if you do not. We pray, Father, "forgive us our debts, as we also have forgiven our debtors" (Matt 6:12 NIV). This means we are actually asking God to forgive us in the same manner and to the same degree that we forgive others. That could get a lot of us who have failed to forgive freely into trouble.

In Luke's gospel the verse reads this way: "Forgive us our sins, for we also forgive everyone who sins against us" (11:4 NIV). This means

> ~~~ The secret to ridding yourself of a root of bitterness is to forgive and release those who have deeply wounded you.

the very justification or grounds on which we ask for forgiveness is that we have forgiven and released *everyone* who has sinned against us. Forgiveness of others is a prerequisite to our own. We are encouraged to be kind and compassionate to others and forgive them, just as in Christ God forgave us. This means we utterly and completely release them as though they owed us nothing.

Essential Forgiveness

For if you forgive men when they sin against you, your heavenly Father will also forgive you. But if you do not forgive men their sins, your Father will not forgive your sins. (Matt. 6:14–15 NIV)

You don't need *Strong's Concordance* to figure this one out. The point is very clear and spoken by Jesus Himself. If you forgive, then your heavenly Father forgives; if you don't forgive, your heavenly Father will not forgive you. The gospel of Mark echoes it again: "But if ye do not forgive, neither will your Father which is in heaven forgive your trespasses" (Mark 11:26 KJV).

This removes all gray areas. Forgiveness is essential if we are to guard our hearts with all diligence. Paul, in one of his letters to the church in Corinth, instructed them from the position of father and apostle of the body of believers there:

> If you forgive anyone, I also forgive him. And what I have forgiven— if there was anything to forgive—I have forgiven in the sight of Christ for your sake, *in order that Satan might not outwit us. For we are not unaware of his schemes.* (2 Cor. 2:10–11 NIV, emphasis added)

What did Satan have to do with Paul's forgiving those whom the saints in Corinth forgave? Because Satan outwits those who are blinded by bitterness and unforgiveness, and Paul wanted to serve as a guard in the spirit for this precious body of believers.

> *Our battle is not with those we can see; we wage war in the realm of the unseen.*

Remember, the Bible is clear: We do not wrestle with people. Our battle is not with those we can see; we wage war in the realm of the unseen that we might walk in peace in the realm of the seen.

THE BATTLE TO FORGIVE

> Put on the full armor of God so that you can take your stand against the devil's schemes. For our struggle is not against flesh and blood, but against the rulers, against the authorities, against the powers of this dark world and against the spiritual forces of evil in the heavenly realms. (Eph. 6:11–12 NIV)

Your real battle is not with the one who has hurt you but with the eternal enemy of your soul. The following Scripture passage grants us further insight into the dark recesses of unforgiveness. Please read it as though you have not read it before, for it holds a precious and important kingdom truth.

> Therefore the kingdom of heaven is like a certain king who wanted to settle accounts with his servants. And when he had begun to settle accounts, one was brought to him who owed him ten thousand talents. But as he was not able to pay, his master commanded that he be sold, with his wife and children and all that he had, and that payment be made. The servant therefore fell down before him, saying, "Master, have patience with me, and I will pay you all." Then the master of that servant was moved with compassion, released him, and forgave him the debt. (Matt. 18:23–27 NKJV)

In our culture we do not understand kings who hold the power of life and death; we have bankruptcy courts to escape our debt. But for a moment, let's travel in this man's shoes. Imagine the terror in your heart as a servant of the king. You have been hearing a rumor for weeks that the king would be settling accounts with his subjects. Now you have received a summons to the palace. You had hoped and prayed that somehow you would be overlooked in all of this. You know you are guilty of mismanaging what was entrusted to you, but you never expected this day to come. You know your debt is great, but long ago you ceased to keep records. One thing is certain: it is a debt you cannot pay.

You wait outside the great throne room until it is your turn to appear before the king. You try to remain calm; perhaps he will give you more time, but your hands are trembling. You are brought before him. Your debt is even more than you had imagined. It is impossible! You don't have the resources. The king orders you to be sold along with your wife, children, and all that you possess, and nods your dismissal. Before the guards can grab you to lead you out, you fall prostrate before this king and beg him to have patience, that somehow you will pay it all. As the guards lift you off the floor the king turns to you again and sees you as a helpless, hopeless man; he thinks of your wife and children. He knows you have mismanaged your debt, but he sees your agony and fear and is moved with compassion. He does not agree to your plea to allow for more time; instead he cancels your debt and tells the guards to release you. Then he rises and leaves the court. Everyone is stunned. You owed more than many others who had gone before you, yet you were freely forgiven.

No one seems to know what to do next. They have just experienced an amazing revelation of the goodness of their king. Mercy has triumphed over just judgment. Still reeling from the revelation that you are free, you begin to laugh then to cry. You hug the stunned guards around you as you leave the great palace. You go home and share the news with your family, and you all rejoice together. An unbelievable and unbearable burden has been released.

Time passes, and the intensity of the king's mercy and your imprisonment has faded from your memory. Yes, you are still thankful; after all, you would not be able to enjoy all that you have if not for the king's kindness. And now you truly do enjoy it because it is completely yours. As time passed you even began to tell yourself that even the king himself must have understood your position and that is why he forgave you. At some level the king must have known you did not deserve such harsh treatment. No longer does debt loom over you like a bad dream. You owe no man anything, but there are those who owe you. You don't ever want to find yourself in such a vulnerable situation again. It is time to collect the debts.

> But that servant went out and found one of his fellow servants who owed him a hundred denarii; and he laid hands on him and took him by the throat, saying, "Pay me what you owe!" So his fellow servant fell down at his feet and begged him, saying, "Have patience with

me, and I will pay you all." And he would not, but went and threw him into prison till he should pay the debt. (Matt. 18:28–30 NKJV)

Isn't it amazing that the fellow servant used the exact words the servant had used with the king when he pleaded for mercy, and still he would not hear him? Not only did he demand payment, but he also grabbed him by the throat, refused to have patience, and threw him into prison until the debt was paid. He exercised to his fullest capacity the judgment he had escaped. How easy it would have been for him to show mercy because he had been shown such great mercy, but he refused. His heart had already hardened to what was done for him.

So when his fellow servants saw what had been done, they were very grieved, and came and told their master all that had been done. Then his master, after he had called him, said to him, "You wicked servant! I forgave you all that debt because you begged me. Should you not also have had compassion on your fellow servant, just as I had pity on you?" And his master was angry, and delivered him to the torturers until he should pay all that was due to him. (Matt. 18:31–34 NKJV)

Notice he is called a *wicked servant*. This man was a servant to the king . . . he just did not have the king's heart. The king had hoped that his goodness would have led this man to repentance and then to compassion for others, but it did not. The king's mercy had been spent in vain, so he reinstated the debt. But this time, instead of being sold, he was turned over to the torturers, to be tormented until he paid in full a debt he could never repay. This man was forgiven only to later be held accountable. But you don't need my opinion; Jesus freely volunteers the interpretation of this parable because He wanted its message clearly portrayed:

So My heavenly Father also will do to you if each of you, from his heart, does not forgive his brother his trespasses. (Matt. 18:35 NKJV)

AN UNPAYABLE DEBT

The king is our heavenly Father, we are the servant with the impossible debt, and our Christian brothers and sisters are the fellow servants. Each of us from our heart *must* forgive the trespasses of others. When we don't forgive we imprison others in the chains

> ✒️ *We are the servant with the impossible debt.*

of guilt and condemnation, and it will not be long before we find ourselves tormented. It may be in this present life or the one to come.

I knew how it felt to live under an unpayable debt. I had accumulated numerous trespasses and offenses on my record when I finally became a Christian. When John led me in a prayer of salvation, he had me repeat after him, "Lord, I confess my sins." I looked at him with panic in my eyes. "I don't know if I can remember them all!" I was afraid the salvation that had come so close would now be lost because of my inexhaustible list.

"No, you don't have to name each one; just confess you have sinned." John assured me that was all that was necessary. I was comforted because I was certain God had kept a much better record of them than I had. I knew I was a sinner, and I knew I needed mercy.

But it wasn't far into my Christian walk before I found myself in a state of unforgiveness with other Christians, or should I say fellow servants. I felt they owed me something like an apology. In the next chapter we are going to discuss in further detail the trap of judging. I allowed this to eat at me. During this time I experienced much spiritual warfare. I constantly felt like a target because I was. I was a Christian who had fallen prey to the schemes of the devil. During this time period I spent a lot of my time in prayer binding and loosing, but to no avail. I was bound by cords of my own making. When I finally saw the truth, I realized it did not matter what was done to me. It didn't matter if I was right and they were wrong. All that mattered was my Lord had commanded me to forgive as I had been forgiven, and I was in disobedience. I was overwhelmed by the extent of my own deception. I

> ✎ I've been bound and I've been free, and free is better.

had thought I was so right when in fact I had been so wrong. I freely forgave and then cried out to the Lord to wash me anew in the cleansing river of His mercy, and He did. I've been bound and I've been free, and free is better. No matter how much humble pie you might have to eat, free is still better than poisoned waters.

How about you? Are you tired of eating the bitter and poisonous fruit produced by a root of bitterness in your life? Then the first step is to be honest and repent. You must turn from hatred and bitterness and allow the Master Gardener to uproot the bitterness from your heart. Though it promised to strengthen and protect you, it has actually drained and violated your position in Christ.

✎ *Dear Heavenly Father,*

I come to You in the name of Jesus. There is bitterness in my heart. While I slept the enemy sowed tares. Separate now the precious from the vile, the life-giving from the life-draining. I renounce the lies of Satan and all his schemes in my life. No longer will I yield to his defiling reasoning. Expose each root and remove it now by Your Spirit. Show me those whom I need to forgive and release. In obedience I set them free from any prison of my making. They owe me nothing. Not even an apology. I place them into Your hands, for You alone are the just Judge.

7 *Big Relief . . .*
You Are Not the Judge

Do not judge, or you too will be judged (Mat. 7:1). What exactly does it mean to judge another? Well, in this reference or connotation it means "to condemn, punish or try." When we are angry or upset with an individual or group, there will always be the temptation to move on to the next level, rage, which

> *Judging is an attempt to absolve ourselves of guilt.*

encourages us to pass judgment. We want to label them because then we can disqualify them as a person or the position they hold. Judging them is also an attempt to absolve ourselves of guilt.

In this book we are dealing with anger firsthand, so it is important to be practical. I believe this means to present something in such a way it can be put into practice.

JUDGING IN DEFENSE

Judging is a defense mechanism. *If anger in its purest form is temporary displeasure, then judgment is permanent rejection.* To illustrate this I'm going to draw again from my long list of failings.

I have already shared how my husband, John, was the one who truly shared Jesus with me. In 1981 we both attended summer school at Purdue University. Though I was a heathen, John had felt very impressed to invite me to a Bible study picnic hosted by one of the professors. This godly couple had opened up their home for years in order to disciple students of which John was just one of many. The Blakes even allowed John to teach at their weekly Bible study so he could grow and develop in a safe and accountable environment. There were many students, including some lovely Christian girls, who attended this study in their home. When John showed up with me, the campus heathen, they all were in shock. Had John backslid? Did he know I was a wild thing? Was I, Satan incarnate, after the leader of their Bible study?

The truth is, I was a college student and a picnic meant free food. I had no initial interest in John whatsoever. He was nice and I didn't date nice boys. I remember feeling like an alien at the picnic. They all seemed to speak the foreign language of Christianese, and I did not understand it. After the meal we all gathered in their living room for a time of worship. I didn't know any of the songs they were singing. Even the music sheets they had passed out with words on them didn't help. I looked around to see if anyone else was as lost as I was. This was an interdenominational gathering and some of the students were raising a hand here and there. I thought to myself, *What is the deal? Do these people have a question?* I was nervous and uncomfortable, so I began to really read the song sheet in earnest. Then the words to one song struck me: "He sees not what I used to be, but He sees Jesus."

> *Could God somehow look at me and not see my sin?*

My mind began to race. Could this be possible? Could God somehow look at me and not see my sin? Could He look at me and not see all the things I had done? I was at once overwhelmed with the awareness of my sin and shame; I wore them both like an uncomfortable garment. I sensed simultaneously the judgment of God and the Spirit's wooing. I turned to John, who was singing. "Is this really true?" I asked pointing to the words. "Could God look at me and not see me?"

John assured me this was true, all the while totally unaware of what was taking place inside me. I began to hear a voice, the one I had always thought was my conscience: "I can't look at you." And I knew why. I was not covered in Christ. I was cloaked in sin and worldliness. This awareness continued to increase as I sensed a strange sort of fear and a battle for my eternal soul.

After the picnic John and I walked the campus for hours, and he shared the gospel with me. For the first time I was able to understand it. All the pieces fit into place. It seemed as if I could see my whole life leading up to that moment. It was intense. I felt I could not wait another moment, so I interrupted John.

"I want to do this. What do I need to do? Do I need a Bible? Do we need to light some candles?"

After making sure I completely understood what I was doing, John prayed with me and I felt as though a five-hundred-pound weight was lifted from my shoulders. I floated back to my dorm room and spent the better part of the night looking for the book of Paul, because John had quoted him so many times; I was certain he had a designated book somewhere. I even assumed he was one of the orig-inal twelve disciples.

The next morning, as I made my bed, God clearly showed me that John was to become my husband. At the time it was just a matter-of-fact sort of thing. I liked John; after all, he had shared the gospel with me and saved my life! But I had always been drawn to wrong men for the wrong reasons. John was quite possibly the first right one to come into my life. As God was dealing with me He was also speaking to John. John asked me to marry him a little more than a month later.

I was certain we would have marital bliss. So certain, in fact, that I had not really bothered to listen when we were in premarriage coun-seling. That type of advice was only necessary for those poor couples who had not been put together by God, not us. More than likely we'd never have any problems. It was only a few short months into our marriage when the conflict started to surface.

The Vision of the Perfect Man

You see, I had a vision of sorts. One, I have since learned, is quite common with newlywed women. It was a vision of a perfect man. This man in my vision looked a lot like John but acted entirely different from John. It was right then as a young newlywed that I found my purpose and embraced my calling in life. I had been handpicked and placed in John's life to change him from who he presently was into the image of this man of vision. A new critical anointing came on my life to accomplish this amazing task. Now, without even trying, I could see my husband's every flaw. I tried to gently persuade at first, and when this failed my tactics became more forceful. I was compelled to guide him in the direction of this perfect man. But John was not cooperating with the process. He was actually resistant. He had visions of his own, ones that involved my transformation. It was then that the fighting began in earnest.

I was trying to change John, and he was trying to change me. Our blissful marriage became a battleground between two very strong-willed people. Sparks flew as the iron attempted to sharpen the iron. Our battles also exposed something else in me. John and I had very different fighting styles. John attacked problems, and I attacked people. This wonderful man who had led me to the Lord was now my problem, and I wasn't fighting fairly. If John hurt me I punished him. I called him names, withheld forgiveness and affection, and broke things. (Remember the plate through the window?) I wanted to hurt him because he'd hurt me. What he did is not the issue here.

When John hurt me I would in turn judge him to alienate him

from that area of my heart in a futile effort to protect myself from future assaults.

For example, if he did something particularly up-setting, I would call him a jerk or some other less-

> ✎ *We will pass judgment on others to try to justify our unforgiveness or rage with them.*

redeemed name. In my mind if I labeled him a jerk, then I did not have to deal with him in that area. My name-calling served to disqualify him or diminish his opinion. If I withheld my affection or forgiveness, it was because I had judged him as unworthy of my love, attention, or forgive-ness at the time. The tragic part is that if enough of these incidents accu-mulate then we are no longer dealing with rejecting isolated areas—we are rejecting the person as an individual. We will pass judgment on others to try to justify our unforgiveness or rage with them.

JUDGE THE ACTIONS, NOT THE HEART

You have heard that it was said to those of old, "You shall not mur-der, and whoever murders will be in danger of the judgment." But I say to you that whoever is angry with his brother without a cause shall be in danger of the judgment. And whoever says to his brother, "Raca!" shall be in danger of the council. But whoever says, "You fool!" shall be in danger of hell fire. (Matt. 5:21–22 NKJV)

Again Jesus drew the parallel between murder and hate. He was show-ing us that under the Law of Moses and this earthly system of justice, murderers are in danger of judgment; then Jesus introduced the king-dom of God perspective. Those angry without a cause are in danger of judgment. Again remember, we have permission to be angry when there is a cause, but never to be destructive or punitive. Then Jesus went on with the progression, giving a practical example: To call a brother "Raca!" put one in danger with the council under Jewish law; under kingdom law, calling someone "You fool!" moved you closer to the flames of hell.

To grasp the meaning of this we must gain an understanding of these words. Matthew Henry's commentary explains it this way: *Raca* "is a scornful word." It

> ∾ *We have permission to be angry when there is a cause, but never to be destructive or punitive.*

means "thou empty fellow"; it speaks of someone void of sense. *Raca* could be used in mild terms to bring someone to his senses. It was an assessment of his behavior as foolish. It was used this way by Jesus, James, and Paul. But if it proceeded from a heart of anger, malice, or slander then it was an affront to the individual. This kind of comment placed the Israelites under discipline by the Sanhedrin for reviling a fellow Israelite.

The term "you fool," on the other hand, was not referring to one without sense but one without grace. It was spiteful and came from hatred. It labeled others as not only mean and not to be honored, but also as vile and not to be loved. It attacked the very spiritual condition of the individual by censuring and condemning them as abandoned by God.

In light of this it is easy to understand why the individual who calls his brother a fool would be in danger of God's judgment, since he has set himself up as the judge of someone's heart and not merely their actions. It is one thing to call someone's actions foolish; it is quite another to label them as rejected by God and unredeemable.

THE CRY FOR JUSTICE

Then why is it so easy to judge and so hard not to? In the first place, as humans made in the image of God we have an inborn desire to see right prevail. The redeemed part of us cries out for justice to be served. God our Father understood this, and it was He who initiated and established the role model for

> ◈ *Why is it so easy to judge and so hard not to?*

our current judicial system: "Appoint judges and officials for each of your tribes in every town the LORD your God is giving you, and they shall judge the people fairly" (Deut. 16:18 NIV).

God knew that anytime more than one person is in a room there is the potential for conflict. He also knew that both sides will dig their heels in and believe they are the ones who are right. Therefore, He made the necessary provision for this. The children of Israel had just left Egyptian bondage, where more than likely they had seen conflict resolved by violence or intimidation. They had yet to see a healthy model of conflict resolution. Isn't that just the place where most of us are?

They had grown up in Egypt under its rules and statutes and were now attempting to live under the cloud of His protec-

> ◈ *God knew that anytime more than one person is in a room there is the potential for conflict.*

tion and presence. But our God is holy and righteous, loving and fearful. He is nothing like the stone images and idols they imagined to be gods before they found the true and living One. Like our God, we must serve in spirit and truth.

So God told Moses through his father-in-law, Jethro, to "select capable men from all the people—men who fear God, trustworthy men who hate dishonest gain—and appoint them as officials over thousands, hundreds, fifties and tens" (Ex. 18:21 NIV). In order to be capable these men had to first fear God and prove themselves to be trustworthy and not interested in any personal gain from their position. Then they were to be appointed over the different divisions of the people.

> *Whenever the LORD raised up a judge for them, he was with the judge* and
> saved them out of the hands of their enemies as long as the judge
> lived; for the LORD had compassion on them as they groaned under
> those who oppressed and afflicted them. (Judg. 2:18 NIV, emphasis
> added)

The Lord God honored these appointments by placing His hand
upon the life of the judge. Whenever God raised up a judge, He was
with him in wisdom and protection. Under the old covenant God
provided His wisdom and will through the structure of these judges. I
believe He placed a measure of His Spirit on these judges that could
comprehend the law and statutes and have the insight necessary to
rightly judge God's people. But these judges appointed by God still
judged only the people's actions and then were faithful executors of
God's will, not their own. They were a pattern and a foreshadowing
of the new way of living Christ brought us into.

Under the new covenant we no longer have the established orders
of judges, but a new Mediator is provided for us.

> And I will ask the Father, and he will give you another Counselor to
> be with you forever—the Spirit of truth. The world cannot accept
> him, because it neither sees him nor knows him. But you know him,
> for he lives with you and will be in you. (John 14:16–17 NIV)

The Battle Not to Judge

It is still a constant battle for us not to judge. We like things in neat
boxes. If we know what fits in each compartment, we are more comfortable, kind of like the Pharisees. I remember being tormented in my
thoughts by a situation that occurred when I had been a Christian for
but a short while. I just couldn't divide it into neat boxes.

There was a Christian couple who traveled and ministered together. They both openly testified how God had joined them in marriage. I had the opportunity to spend time with both of them and felt that they both genuinely loved God and His people. Suddenly there were all sorts of ugly rumors, and before you knew it these two were in the throes of a divorce. There had been no adul-

> *It is still a constant battle for us not to judge.*

tery; it just seemed they weren't compatible after all. This really threw me for a loop. I was struggling with issues in my marriage and was trusting God to work them out because I was certain He had brought John and me together. Yet, this couple, who had also said God had put them together, had bailed out on their marriage, and the wife quickly married someone else.

This shook my confidence that God could do something in my marriage. I felt compelled to find some type of fault with this couple. If I could disqualify them, I could squeeze them into a box. After all, I could find Scriptures to justify my position: The Bible says if any divorce for reasons other than unfaithfulness, they become adulterers. Yet I just wasn't comfortable labeling this couple as adulterers. I loved them and wanted to understand, but I could not make sense of the whole issue.

Without using any names I poured out the turmoil in my heart to a wise and godly minister. I braced myself for a long, in-depth biblical explanation. But instead he just sighed and said, "That's a tough one. I'm glad I don't have to judge it."

Immediately I felt the weight of the situation lift from me. His simple words had set me free from my burden. He was right. I had allowed Satan to stir my heart to judge others and then doubted the faithfulness of God to me. I was measuring my marriage by theirs and limiting God to what He could do in mine. In this case I was not judging out of anger but out of fear.

A number of years ago, John and I took a group of young people down to Trinidad to join forces with a local church and witness in the streets and from house to house. It was immediately after the Jimmy Swaggart and Jim Bakker scandals, and we encountered questions as to the integrity of these men everywhere we turned. At first it threw us. Then I had the revelation, *Wait a minute! Neither Jimmy Swaggart or Jim Bakker has anything to do with what we are preaching.* I was able to answer back boldly, "Those men did not die for your sins, Jesus did. They have nothing to do with what we are saying . . . stop making excuses."

We will often judge others to reduce the pressure from ourselves. When I fought with John I was very hard on him. But do you know who I was the hardest on? Myself. I attacked John to justify and deflect the detection of my own flaws. If I could establish him as imperfect, I did not have to feel so badly that I was not perfect. The only problem is that whenever you judge, you place yourself under judgment.

> So when you, a mere man, pass judgment on them and yet do the same things, do you think you will escape God's judgment? Or do you show contempt for the riches of his kindness, tolerance and patience, not realizing that God's kindness leads you towards repentance? (Rom. 2:3–4 NIV)

The very thing we accuse others of, as mere men we also do. The very thing we are trying to avoid, we end up bringing upon ourselves.

> ✒ *The very thing we are trying to avoid, we end up bringing upon ourselves.*

We judge to safeguard ourselves from injury or criticism, but each and every one of us is guilty. God tells us that by judging others we are, in fact, showing contempt for His mercy and kindness. He then reminds us that it was His kindness that brought us to repentance.

Even though we live in a culture that has set up judges, we must heed Paul's admonishment to the Christians to behave differently.

> I say this to shame you. Is it possible that there is nobody among you wise enough to judge a dispute between believers? But instead, one brother goes to law against another—and this in front of unbelievers! The very fact that you have lawsuits among you means you have been completely defeated already. Why not rather be wronged? Why not rather be cheated? (1 Cor. 6:5–7 NIV)

Notice, we are still allowed to judge disputes, but Paul encouraged the body of believers to pick wise arbitrators from among them so their case would not come before a heathen court of nonbelievers. But his greatest concern was there would even be a lawsuit among them. He would rather have them wronged by another brother than to go to such lengths to assert their rights.

Again it is like my fighting with my husband. It is all right for me to bring up issues as long as I attack the problem and not the person. Initially this takes a lot of practice. We have to learn to catch ourselves. In my personal experience I have found I am often quicker to defend myself than catch myself. Therefore, I am not always the most reliable judge of my own behavior. I need the intercession of One much wiser and more impartial to the situation.

THE PROBLEM WITH PRIDE

> Pride only breeds quarrels, but wisdom is found in those who take advice. (Prov. 13:10 NIV)

My pride would often keep me from backing down even when I knew I was wrong. If pride is the breeding ground for quarrels, then humility is the womb for reconciliation. Whenever I have humbled myself, I have witnessed healing and forgiveness when these looked impossible. There are many ways to be humbled, but judging others is not one of them. When we judge others we are not abasing ourselves but exalting ourselves as superior in position, insight, or intelligence.

> _If pride is the breeding ground for quarrels, then humility is the womb for reconciliation._

The greatest testimony of all is for us to walk in love and forgiveness, not exercising our rights over one another. This only happens when we allow the Holy Spirit to intervene on our behalf and repent of the tendency to set ourselves up as judges.

In the next chapter we are going to address an issue that is important to have settled. It is tempting to believe that we are judged. It is my prayer that every area of judgment will be lifted from your life.

> You, then, why do you judge your brother? Or why do you look down on your brother? For we will all stand before God's judgment seat. (Rom. 14:10 NIV)

Dear Heavenly Father,

I come before You in the name of Jesus. I repent of bowing to the pressure and trap of judging others. Forgive me and wash me clean. Release any areas in my life where this has placed me under Your judgment or the judgment of man. I humble myself and repent of pride and foolishness. Your mercy alone triumphs over judgment, and I now humbly ask for Your mercy to cover my mistakes and unveil my eyes. I want truth, not suspicion. I want the holy fear of the Lord, not the fear of man. Shine the light of Your truth in any areas of my darkness.

8 Is God Angry at Women?

This may seem an odd question to ask in a book addressing the topic of personal anger *in* women. But I believe it is always difficult to let go of our anger when we feel that we are the target or subject of someone else's.

Before I was saved I always envisioned God up in the clouds with a tally card that contained a record of all my follies and sins. Every transgression had an X-mark by it accordingly. He was upset and totally prepared to throw me into hell. I felt as if there were no possible avenues of reconciliation left. I had sinned repeatedly, and there was no way to erase my dark deeds.

Imagine my shock when John shared that God had told him to ask me out. To even grasp that God might be thinking somewhat remotely about

> ➤ *It is always difficult to let go of our anger when we feel that we are the target or subject of someone else's.*

me outside of plans for my inevitable judgment was a surprise, to say the least. Then to hear that He loved me . . . it was too much for me to comprehend. In response to such beautiful mercy, I abandoned myself to His care. I never even thought of my femininity as an issue.

Then I went to churches, conferences, and assorted meetings where I heard things that clouded the issue of His love for me. Somehow I was getting the impression that I had slipped into redemption as a second-class citizen of the kingdom. Now mind you, I don't believe anyone ever said it straight-out, but it was an undercurrent nonetheless: Women were not to be trusted and barely redeemed.

A GODLY WOMAN?

My first confusing encounter happened while I was still in college. I traveled from Arizona to Houston to attend a Thanksgiving seminar. I had been saved all of four months and was so excited and anxious to join those of precious, like faith and hear liberating truths from the Word of God. It had been a lonely struggle for me. I desperately wanted to be pleasing to my heavenly Father, so I opened my heart and got out my pen, paper, and new Bible with my name engraved on the front. But I was not prepared for what I was about to hear. After a time of worship during which I wept, the pastor got up and opened in prayer then encouraged everyone to sit down. He called his wife up to the platform. I leaned forward to catch a closer glimpse of this woman. I needed a role model; perhaps I could glean something even from this distance.

I watched as a gracious and lovely woman ascended a platform encircled by thousands. As she stood by her husband he began a series of jokes and put-downs, all of which she was the brunt of. She answered a few back in jest also. The congregation laughed, but I felt a bit sick. His cuts seemed to dig a little deeper than hers did. It was as though she knew her limits, and he had none. I was soon to find out why.

"Do you know where we men would be without women?" he asked genially, addressing the congregation. I began to think in earnest of an answer. I imagined he was now going to say something nice after all the put-downs of her intelligence and worth.

"Men would still be in the Garden." The whole place erupted in laughter. I scanned the audience. Both men and women were laughing. Was I the only one uncomfortable and confused by the comment? Had I come out of one world of shame to be made fun of in another? I looked at the married couple sitting with John and me. They were laughing. I looked at John. He could sense I was confused and disturbed. My face went hot, and I felt tears trying to escape my eyes. I turned to John and said, "I'm going to the rest room." I walked out feeling conspicuous, as though I had the banner of an outcast and rebel draped across my shoulders.

In the ladies' room as I looked around again, it appeared that I was the only one upset by the comment. It was probably something I just needed to get over. I returned to the service and took notes in earnest, but something was missing. His words remained just letters on my notepad. My trust was violated, and I was afraid to allow his message into my heart.

In the car on the way home I asked a friend of mine if the pastor and his wife always treated each other like that. She said that they did and assured me they were just joking around. John and I were newly engaged, and I was having second thoughts about Christian couples. I wanted something more than that.

The next day, instead of joining John in the service, I made excuses and volunteered in the nursery. I was more comfortable believing God loved me as I comforted and rocked crying infants. As I held them and watched them respond to my gentle voice in the face of their piercing cries, I imagined this was how God felt about me.

> *Inside I was screaming and He was speaking gently to me.*

Inside I was screaming and He was speaking gently to me. I was His daughter; He was my Father. Tears welled again in my eyes as I rocked the sleeping infant. There was so much I didn't understand, but His love was certain.

A Godly Marriage?

Then after John and I had been married a few months, a wealthy couple in the church invited us to their home for dinner. I thought it was unusual at the time, but it appeared that they wanted to mentor John and me in the ways of marriage. We were all sitting together in the living room before dinner. Anytime I asked a question or interjected a comment, I was completely ignored. I would say or ask something, but the husband would say, "So, John, what do you think about . . ." and totally change the subject. At first I thought he was hard of hearing or that it was an accident. Then I realized it was intentional. John even tried to include me in the conversation, but our host would have none of it. After a while his wife slipped silently from her position at his feet and went into the kitchen. Confused, I followed her.

"Is there anything I can help with?" I offered, because I felt so totally, purposely ignored.

"No, I have everything taken care of," she answered sweetly but firmly. I had obviously done or said something she did not approve of. I became more uncomfortable and started to think maybe being quiet in the living room was a better option than being useless in the kitchen. I ventured closer to the exit of their well-appointed kitchen.

"Stay in here!" she barked at me.

I turned around, slightly surprised. What was the deal? I couldn't help in the kitchen *or* talk in the living room? I watched as this woman decked in jewels and designer clothes basted her *coq au vin*. She was in her late forties or early fifties; I was twenty-two. In an irritated and measured tone she began to tell me the way it was.

"You are not to speak to the men unless you are spoken to. Your place is in the kitchen with me."

I was slightly shocked. Was I hearing her correctly? I must have looked dumbfounded, so she asked me point-blank: "Do you want a good marriage or not?"

This only served to further confuse me. I had only been married two or three months. I was no expert, but we barely had a marriage at this point let alone a bad one. I did want to be a good wife. "Yes, I want a good marriage," I stammered back foolishly.

She shoved the chicken back into the oven and ordered me to sit down. I fought back the temptation to ask how much longer before the chicken was ready and obediently sat down. She told me many things that night—things God had supposedly taught her. Some were so foolish, sexual, and distasteful I will not even bother repeating them on these pages. But here is a sampling: I was told to always sit lower than my husband. If he was on a chair I was to sit on the floor. (I wasn't sure how this was going to happen at the dining table since all the chairs appeared to be the same height.) I realized I had already violated that one by daring to sit alongside my husband on the sofa when we first arrived. So that was why no one would answer me! She continued with more wisdom. If I ever thought of speaking back to my husband, I was to immediately find a toilet and fall on my knees in front of it. This was to serve the purpose of reminding me just what my position in life was and arrest any of my foolish outbursts before they even began. I had only kneeled in front of a toilet when I had been nauseated and I was fearing a relapse right about then.

Sex was reduced to a duty that did not necessarily include my pleasure. I got a little radical and dared to challenge her advice in this area.

"Why would God make both sexes capable of enjoying sex if He only wanted the males to?"

"You are to do 'it' whenever your husband wants 'it' whether you enjoy it or not!" she retorted.

"After a while wouldn't you resent it?" I asked.

"Then you go back to the toilet," she explained.

Wow, I could see already under her regimen I would be spending a lot of time in front of the toilet. I decided it was best not to argue anymore. This woman was serious!

Mercifully dinner was ready, and John and I sat uncomfortably where they placed us. I was severely quiet during the dinner, trying to avoid any further violations. John seemed a little uncomfortable too. I was beginning to dread what he had been asked or educated in while I was being grilled in the kitchen. We excused ourselves quickly after the meal and ran through sleety rain to our cold car. There was an incredible heaviness over both of us.

"John, that was really weird. Did you notice how I wasn't allowed to talk and how rude he was?"

John seemed deep in thought. "Yeah, it was sort of strange, but maybe he just wanted to talk man to man with me."

"Well, there are ways to do that without being rude," I countered.

"What did he ask you about when you were alone with him?" I probed.

"Lots of things," John answered.

"Did he ask you any questions about me personally . . . I mean sexually?" I asked, half afraid and half embarrassed.

"Yes, it was strange," John replied.

"I think they're weird. How dare they separate us and ask about our personal life!" I declared.

"They are a prominent, wealthy couple in the church. They are just trying to be nice." Was John really defending them or was he just as confused as I was?

I went to bed with dread all over me. What if this marriage thing had all been a trick to put me into some kind of unbelievable bondage? Did other Christian women live by these rules? Maybe it was like my sorority, and this was initiation time when all the secret rituals and meanings came out. John seemed a little distant. Maybe he had arranged for the wife to talk to me. After all, it was a great arrangement for the males. My overly active brain went into high gear, and I was a slave by morning.

When I woke the next morning John had already left for work. I hurried and got ready to go to work at my position in the church's accounting department. I felt so heavy and hopeless, I started to cry on the way to work and couldn't stop. I cried the entire morning at my desk. If anyone asked me what was wrong, I just shook my head. Finally my boss called me in.

"Lisa, you have been crying all morning. What in heaven's name is wrong with you?"

Before I could contain it, I told her every detail except for the names of the couple who had invited us to dinner. She listened in disbelief, but I wasn't sure whether it was disbelief of my reaction to it or to what I was telling her.

"Stay right here and try to pull yourself together," she said and excused herself. She returned a few minutes later with the pastor's wife. Now I was terrified, but I didn't need to be.

"Who told you all this nonsense?" she asked.

I hesitated, remembering their position in the church. I was just a poor new member, and these were people who had money to burn.

"I want to know who did this!" she demanded. I told her and she was furious. She explained that they were brand-new Christians themselves and in no position to be teaching anyone. They had only been married a year or two, and she was his third wife and he was her second husband. "Just because they have money doesn't make them an expert in the things of God!" I guess the toilet plan didn't work because within two years this couple divorced.

> My opinion does not matter; God's Word is the final authority.

I have given two examples of abuse of women with the presumed backing of God. One is mild, the other severe. Unfortunately both are all too common. Why do women laugh when cutting remarks are leveled against their gender from the very leaders they look to for training, protection, and guidance? Is it because they are afraid not to?

No, I am afraid it goes even deeper. They believe it is true at some level and therefore they deserve the abuse.

If I have learned anything, it is this: My opinion does not matter; God's Word is the final authority. Is God mad at women? Does the Creator of the universe harbor some unresolved offense toward women? In answer let's go to His Word.

A LOVING HUSBAND

"For your Maker is your husband—the LORD Almighty is his name—the Holy One of Israel is your Redeemer; he is called the God of all the earth. The LORD will call you back as if you were a wife deserted and distressed in spirit—a wife who married young, only to be rejected," says your God. "For a brief moment I abandoned you, but with deep compassion I will bring you back. In a surge of anger I hid my face from you for a moment, but with everlasting kindness I will have compassion on you," says the LORD your Redeemer. "To me this is like the days of Noah, when I swore that the waters of Noah would never again cover the earth. So now I have sworn not to be angry with you, never to rebuke you again. Though the mountains be shaken and the hills be removed, yet my unfailing love for you will not be shaken nor my covenant of peace be removed," says the LORD, who has compassion on you. (Isa. 54:5–10 NIV)

Our marvelous Father compares His redemption of us to the love of a husband for his wife. He could have said, "Your Maker is Your Father," but He did not. He positions Himself as a loving husband restoring a wayward wife. He then compares the surety of His promise to the one He made to Noah: "Though the mountains be shaken and the hills be removed, yet my unfailing love for you will not be shaken nor my covenant of peace be removed." No matter how intense the shaking in your life, God's love for you will never waver. Let this issue be settled once and forever in your mind.

This Scripture does not carry a disclaimer with it. This promise is for all! It does not exclude women who are single, divorced, barren, or widowed. This promise spans all age-groups as well. It is spoken in affectionate and tender terms a woman would understand. It is the voice of God speaking to His beloved and precious ones. He is speaking peace to His women. So receive His peace and let it still your anger and fear.

Women are granted a unique opportunity. Everything about us is created to serve and nurture. But when we live under the constant fear of displeasure from our heavenly Father, we become weary in well-doing. We fear that no effort will ever be good enough, no sacrifice ever great enough. Remember, it is based not on what you do but on what was done for you. None of us could ever live a life pleasing enough to satisfy all the statutes. We must be women after His heart. But we will not pursue Him if we fear rejection and His wrath. This creates an atmosphere rife with frustration and

> ✺ *Receive His peace and let it still your anger and fear.*

inevitably anger. God wants to release His daughters from this heavy burden. It will weigh you down and set you perpetually on edge.

The mere fact that Jesus is coming back for His bride again reinforces God's tender love for women. If we were lower than a counterpart and completer for man, God would not have chosen the intimate relationship between a man and his wife to illustrate the great mystery of Christ and the church.

✺ *Heavenly Father,*

I come to You in the precious name of Jesus. I realize that I have allowed a lie to creep in and rob from our relationship. If You said it, I believe it. I do believe that You are and that You are true, good, and just.

Please remove any trace of the lie that You are somehow angry with me because I am a woman. I am a woman by Your divine design and purpose. It is not something to be resented or ashamed of. It is something to be celebrated because I am fearfully and wonderfully made. Wash away all the shame, guilt, and stereotypes from my mind. Renew in me a right spirit and impress upon my spirit what manner of woman you would have me to be. I forgive those who have maligned me through prejudice in ignorance; they did not know what they were doing. Lord, restore and reconcile men and women so that we might live in the fruitful garden of Your love once again.

9 Born Angry

I think I was born angry . . . or should I say passionate and ready? My mother told me of a time when I was one or two. To prevent me from freezing, she brought me in from the snow before I was ready to come in. In protest I sat down, spread my legs, and banged my head repeatedly on the floor. Fearing possible brain damage, my mother rushed me to the safety of my crib where I continued my outburst in comfort.

There was another more frightening time when I was throwing a temper tantrum of gargantuan proportions. She had put me in the crib, and somehow I threw myself out of it. I had been screaming for more than twenty minutes when she called our family doctor. He recommended that she vacate the house by stepping outside onto the back porch for a few minutes. He felt the tantrum was being thrown for her benefit and would cease if she left. My mother followed his advice and allowed me the opportunity to perform my fit to an empty house. The hope was that I would then model constructive behavior to retrieve the attention I had lost.

But I greatly failed the test. Apparently when I realized I was alone I became even more enraged. I mustered all the strength and height my two-year-old body could afford and proceeded to pull down everything in the house within my reach. I toppled every dining room chair. Not satisfied with this alone, I kicked out each seat as well. My destructive rampage included pulling all the cushions off the sofa, tossing every ashtray, and overturning every basket. Magazines were thrown helter-skelter, and every bit of order within my reach was changed to disorder. This was not the haphazard act of a slightly upset toddler. It was more like the methodical, destructive force of a pre-school terrorist!

My mother came in from a few moments of solitude on the back porch and found me spent of strength but still furious. Afraid I was possibly resting in preparation for another round, she spanked me soundly and put me to bed!

What was I so ticked off about anyway? Well, let's talk about my heritage. Maybe some blame can be placed in that arena. I'm half Sicilian, as well as Apache, French, and English. Of course I couldn't help but be born passionate and upset. I have Mafia vendettas coursing through my veins, and somebody stole my land! For all I know I could be a direct descendant of Geronimo! Then mingle this with the blood of English- and Frenchmen, and I am coexisting with my invaders!

Add to this equation the fact I'd lost an eye to cancer at the age of five. When they told me they were going to take out my eye and give me a shiny new one, I was not very cooperative. I tried to escape from the hospital before the surgery. I had to be sedated and then fought so hard they couldn't get me to go under. I remember they had me count to ten and I did it twice. Then they fitted me with an even tighter mask and blackness overtook me. I pleaded with them in my sleep all through the surgery, begging them not to take my eye. One nurse left the surgery in tears. I was wheeled into a glass-walled recovery room off to the side. I awoke long before I was supposed to, sat up and ripped the patch off my eye, threw up, and started yelling. I was sedated again.

So much anesthesia had been used to get me under that I developed pneumonia. I awoke freezing and cold in an oxygen tent. After nearly a month in the ward at Riley's Children's Hospital, I returned to kindergarten with a patch over my eye. I was teased and made fun of even after the patch was removed and my eye was fitted with the prosthesis.

ANGER AS ARMOR

Anger became my armor, a force of strength in my life. Vengeful thoughts and images became my solace. I dreamed of someday receiving an eye transplant and becoming whole and normal again. Then no one would dare to make fun of me.

It didn't happen the way I had planned, but when I became a Christian I found wholeness not by returning to my former physical state but by exchanging my old way of life for His new. For a while after becoming a Christian, it seemed none of the old me had survived the transition. I was so overwhelmingly aware of the mercy I had received that I was quick to extend mercy to others.

> *I was so overwhelmingly aware of the mercy I had received that I was quick to extend mercy to others.*

Time passed and I got married, had a vision and a calling, and encountered an uncooperative spouse. I have already shared how our first four years of marriage were filled with fighting.

Then I had my first child. This brought with it another revelation. I discovered it was much easier to love my baby than my husband of three years. When I first saw this little one, beat up and bruised from a forceps delivery, my heart swelled with overwhelming and protective love for our sweet, tender little boy. I had a rough recovery from my labor, which kept me in bed for two weeks. I would lie on my bed with him next to me and just stare at him. I talked to him and believed he actually understood me. I made up all sorts of silly songs that declared my love for him. One memory is especially dear to me. I was lying on my side and had positioned him on his side so that we were nose to nose. I was staring into his serene eyes, and without realizing it, drifted off into the most peaceful and wonderful sleep. I'm not certain how long it lasted, but when I awoke he was still staring at me with such love that it overwhelmed me. It was as though a little cherub were watching over me. I kissed him wildly all over his sweet little face.

John was not quite as enraptured with the whole experience. He was feeling a little left out. Or was it possibly something else? I accused him of being jealous when he would make comments such as "Hasn't that baby been nursing long enough?"

How horrid, I thought. *He is jealous of his own son.* But that was not altogether the truth. You see, he watched me sing to the baby, hold the baby, kiss the baby, protect the baby, and realized, *Hey, she does know how to be nice. She just refuses to be nice to me!*

He was right. I did treat Addison very differently from the way I treated John. After all, I reasoned, he was an adult and could fend for himself. This child was mine to love and protect all the days of his life. The first two years of Addison's life brought many changes and transitions for us. We moved from Texas to Florida, where John had taken a position as a youth pastor for a local church. And God had begun a tremendous work in our marriage.

All these changes created a deep hunger in my life for God. I wanted to hear His voice clearly, and I wanted to learn His ways. Part of this was because of the position I was now in. As a pastor's wife I wanted to be a godly example. But I cannot say my motivations were completely pure. God had healed my marriage, and I was sitting on the front row of the church. I reasoned God must be pretty pleased with me or I would not be enjoying this position. Wrong!

Regardless of my self-serving, self-righteous motivation, God gave me the desires of my heart, but by a very different process. I cried out to Him and asked Him to cleanse my heart and bring me deeper into His holy presence. I thought a dream or a vision would be nice. Maybe even something that I would one day testify about and could also serve the purpose of affirming my godliness, but no such luck.

God knows the prescribed procedure and purpose to use in the refining process in each believer's life. I am afraid in my case that meant furnace turned up to high and timer set for more than a year. When gold or silver is refined it is put in the fire at high temperatures until it liquefies. Then the dross and impurities rise to the surface and become apparent to all who witness the process. The metallurgist at this point skims off the dross and then allows the metal to cool again. This process is then repeated until the precious metal is free of contaminants and alloys that will weaken it.

THE REFINING FIRE

See, I have refined you, though not as silver; I have tested you in the furnace of affliction. (Isa. 48:10 NIV)

God does not refine His children in a literal furnace of fire. He has a furnace of another sort that accomplishes this refining process. It is the furnace of affliction. I think it is important at this point to define *affliction*. It means "hardship, trouble, adversity, distress, and trial," to name a few. I especially like the word *hardship*. I would imagine it has its origins in the description of a difficult passage on a vessel at sea. It is a vessel of no escape on which you are being transported from one port to another. You like where you are going, but you do not like the process!

Likewise, a furnace is a place of no escape. There is no interior release handle. Therefore, you might as well get refined as quickly as possible because you are not departing the process until you have achieved the desired state of purity. I believe with all my heart that God is more concerned with our condition than our comfort and He will allow things to become uncomfortable in our lives to expose our true condition. He would rather have us temporarily uncomfortable than eternally tormented.

It seemed that no sooner had I prayed to God to cleanse my heart than I found myself in a fiery furnace of affliction. There had been a

> ✖ *God is more concerned with our condition than our comfort.*

minor problem in my life that was about to become major. It was a private and personal one. It was not something that I did in public or at church; it was something that I saved for my loved ones at home. It was just a little problem with anger.

Now in all truth I was not, at that point, altogether convinced I even had a problem with anger. After all, when everyone was perfect, I wasn't angry; therefore imperfect people made me mad. Furthermore, these outbursts were not daily occurrences. Maybe once every couple of months I might break something or call my husband names. It wasn't like it was out of hand or anything. The time of the broken window incident was immediately following my prayer . . . almost as if in answer to it. But how could I possibly be getting worse as a result of an earnest prayer to be godly? There must be something else stirring it up.

My uncontrollable outbursts increased in frequency. Now they were once a month. About that time information came out about PMS. I had my answer! When I had my first son, something strange and frightening had happened to my hormones. What a relief to have something to blame. I sat my husband down and read him the article. If I could educate him, he could be more sensitive to the changes taking place in my body. I even backed it with the practice in many cultures of isolating menstruating women. After all, even the Bible recommended that men not even sit on the sofa with them!

Then my outbursts seemed to jump from once a month to a couple of times of month. And, besides, the PMS theory was working against me. If I was in the throes of some passionate argument for my rights, John would inevitably ask, "Are you about to start your period?" This served to negate the validity of my case. I had to come up with another solution.

Our youth group was growing. Eureka! The witches in Orlando were fasting and praying against us. I was under spiritual attack, and warfare was being waged in the heavenlies. With all this going on, of course it was understandable that I would be on edge.

Then I heard about the sins of the fathers. Well with my heritage, of course this was to blame. All things considered I should be even worse. Then there was my upbringing. My parents were divorced twice, and my father had a drinking problem. The rage fits came closer and closer together, not unlike a woman in labor. Yet even with all my excuses I was afraid of what I might do!

Then I had my second child. I had prayed and prayed for another little one, and when it happened I thought, *What was I thinking!* One child is so easy. They are kind of like an accessory. You dress them up, you take them out for everyone to admire in their stroller, and they behave well. I realized then it was all a trick to get you to have more children. I was so discouraged, feeling trapped at home with a newborn and a toddler. Not that I could have gone anywhere if I had a car. I seemed incapable of brushing my teeth before noon, and the very thought of going to the grocery store with two children just about pushed me over the edge! I didn't seem able to accomplish anything around the house either. It had never been so messy. I had more time at home than I'd ever had before, yet I accomplished less in more time than I ever had in my life! My mind seemed to be clouded with a postpartum haze. Perhaps there had been a major brain cell drain during my recent pregnancy.

Every night, without fail, my husband would come home to chaos and ask the question, the one I had learned to dread more than any other: "What did you do all day?"

Frustrated, I would stammer back some weak defense and promise I hadn't even watched TV! I would share how the phone had been ringing all day with counseling calls and one girl threatening suicide when I was tempted to join. I must have been a terrifying mess standing there with my nursing flaps down, an infant on my hip, and a spank spoon in my hand. "If you will just hold him for fifteen minutes I will take a shower," I'd promise desperately.

There was a new obstacle between me and what might have been deemed a successful day. My firstborn son, the very one who had been the picture of obedience and compliance, was now fighting me at every turn. Naps had become a major point of contention. No sooner had Austin arrived than Addison decided naps were no longer going to be a viable part of his daily schedule. He was afraid he might be missing something if he dared to sleep for a mere hour or two.

Every day I waged the same battle because I did not agree with his assessment. Naps were a good and necessary part of his daily routine. It was the time period when Mommy took a shower, cleaned the kitchen, and did whatever was necessary to avoid flunking the dreaded question again, "What did you do all day?"

But I was losing ground quickly. It didn't matter how tired he was or how nicely I read to him—he felt compelled to get off his bed. I would nurse Austin and lay him in the cradle in our room and escort Addison upstairs. Everything would be in place; he would be kissed and read to or sung to, and then I would attempt my escape. More often than not, no sooner was I down the stairs than I would turn to find him pattering after me, armed with a list of reasons why he didn't need to nap. At first I remained calm and escorted him back to his bed with warnings against further infractions. But then the phone would ring and he would snap into action. He knew I was trapped downstairs (this was before the cordless phone) and would creep out of his room and into the loft to play with his toys.

I would catch a glimpse of him in the loft from the kitchen and begin to stomp my foot, snap my fingers, and frantically wave a spank spoon at him. He would graciously wave back and continue with his project. The person on the line more often than not had called for counseling and had no idea what this scene in my home looked like. They probably envisioned me as serene, seated in the middle of a Bible study or prayer, when in fact I looked like a banshee mother in a bathrobe waving a spoon above my head as if performing some kind of unknown parental ritual.

When I hung up the phone Addison would run back to the safety of his bed . . . for a moment. Usually he would pass out somewhere between the top of the stairs and his bed, but it seemed that his sleep would in turn trigger a wake-up response in my infant. His tender cries would cause my milk to let down, and I had lost again.

This battle continued from April until July. Then one day I snapped. It was as though I no longer even saw my son; I saw an enemy—the one who kept me from getting anything finished. He was on his way down the stairs, and before I knew it I found myself racing to meet his descent. I picked him up and stormed upstairs. I entered his room and desperately wondered what I could do so that he would not get off his bed again. Without putting him down I carried him over to his bed. It was then that a thought came to me.

Lift him to eye level, slam him into the wall above his bed, and place him on the bed. Then he will know not to get up again. The strange part is, at that moment the thought made sense. I lifted him eye to level, and at that moment I caught a glimpse of the look in his eyes. There was something there I had never seen before. He was not afraid of what I was going to do . . . he was afraid of me! And when I saw the terror in his eyes, I remembered my own when I was a child.

As I previously mentioned, I was a difficult child growing up under difficult conditions. My parents were not Christians, and they raised me the best they knew how. But neither of them had enjoyed a Christian upbringing, and I eventually pushed them to the edge. Now as I saw my son's fear I remembered the promise I had made to myself as a child. "I will never treat my children this way." This jolted me back to my senses.

I gently lowered Addison to his bed and looked deeply into his eyes. "Mommy is so sorry she scared you," I voiced repeatedly, hoping to somehow restore whatever I had violated. Then I closed his door behind me and ran downstairs. I threw myself onto the open expanse of carpeting in my living room and sobbed under the whole, hopeless weight of it all.

I don't know how long I wept, but I cried until I was spent of strength and a stillness settled over me. Through eyes blurred by tears, I saw for the first time that my rage was a problem. My mind revisited the question John had repeatedly asked me after one of my temper tantrums:

> *What's it going to take for you to get a grip on this anger?*

"What's it going to take for you to get a grip on this anger?"

I had always been so quick to answer in defense, "If you wouldn't push me I wouldn't be so angry." But John was not home, nor had he pushed me, and I had almost lost it. For the first time my rage was exacting a price I was not willing to pay. I had violated my son's trust and the promises of my youth. I was not willing to remain the same but had no idea how to break free from this destructive cycle I found myself spiraling into.

I alone was to blame. It wasn't my upbringing, my husband, my ethnic background, or my hormones. Yes, those things and events had forged and fashioned certain areas of my life, but I alone was responsible for my response to them. I cried out to the silence now shrouding my house, "God, it's me! I have a real problem with anger!"

I felt trapped in a swirling whirlpool of my mistakes and excuses. I felt as if I would drown in the sorrowful pool of my own making. Broken and desperate, I cried out for help. "God, I don't want this anymore. I will no longer justify it or blame anyone else. Please forgive me!"

In response I felt the weight of guilt and sin removed from me as though an unseen and heavy garment had been lifted from my entire being. Then I heard the Spirit say, *Because you are no longer justifying this . . . I will take it out of your life.*

WHAT YOU JUSTIFY, YOU BUY

By justifying your anger, you are in essence saying, "I have earned the right to be this way because of what was done to me." You are not defined by what was done to you . . . but by what was done for you! Many people in the body of Christ are still trapped in the abuses of their past when a way of liberty and escape has been provided. Our freedom is found when we follow the instructions of Jesus: "Then he said to them all: 'If anyone would come after me, he must deny himself and take up his cross daily and follow me'" (Luke 9:23 NIV).

> *Our freedom is found when we follow the instructions of Jesus.*

The precursor to taking up your cross is denying yourself. I was not denying myself; I was excusing and justifying myself. I was wandering down a path of destruction paved with faulty stones of my own counsel. When my eyes were opened, I saw the error of my ways. When I repented and denied myself, He in turn delivered me.

LIVE BY THE SPIRIT

So I say, live by the Spirit, and you will not gratify the desires of the sinful nature. For the sinful nature desires what is contrary to the

Spirit, and the Spirit what is contrary to the sinful nature. They are in conflict with each other, so that you do not do what you want. (Gal. 5:16–17 NIV)

There is a conflict between life in the Spirit and our base sinful nature. The only way to resolve this conflict is to live by the Spirit.

> ✒ When I repented and denied myself, He in turn delivered me.

What did I want? I wanted to be a great wife and mother, as well as a godly woman. But because I was not living by the Spirit, I was doing what I did not want.

Life by the Spirit is found when we deny ourselves, take up our cross, and follow Him. I believe taking up our cross represents a laying down of our will. It is when we repeat the words of our Lord: "Yet not what I will, but what you will" (Mark 14:36 NIV).

Life in the Spirit breaks the power of the law over our lives: "But if you are led by the Spirit, you are not under law" (Gal. 5:18 NIV). Under the law it is an eye for an eye and a tooth for a tooth. You hurt me, I'll hurt you. I was abused, therefore I will abuse. There is not a whole lot of hope under the law, yet I find most Christians more eager to excuse and place themselves under the law than under the Spirit. By excusing our present with our past, we negate a major portion of the work of the Cross. It becomes a blame game. God makes each of us in His image, with a free will to choose life or death, blessing or cursing.

> The acts of the sinful nature are obvious: sexual immorality, impurity and debauchery; idolatry and witchcraft; hatred, discord, jealousy, fits of rage, selfish ambition, dissensions, factions and envy; drunkenness, orgies, and the like. I warn you, as I did before, that those who live like this will not inherit the kingdom of God. (Gal. 5:19–20 NIV)

There it was in black and white, and I was busted. God clearly labels fits of rage as an act of the sinful nature. Other translations call it a work of the flesh. Witchcraft is even listed as a work of the flesh. So much for my spiritual warfare excuse. I was wrestling with my own unsubmitting, fallen nature. I want to highlight the final line

> ✺ *A habit is something we do without thinking.*

of this Scripture. Paul said, "I warn you, as I did before, that *those who live like this* will not inherit the kingdom of God." Notice, he said, "those who live like this." Another translation reads, "those who practice such things." There is a vast difference between isolated incidents of sin and a lifestyle or practice of sin. When a doctor finishes his internship, it is time to set up a practice, a place where he will practice medicine day in and day out. Another word for *practice* is *habit*, and a habit is something we do without thinking.

I believe Paul is citing these works of the flesh as habitual lifestyles or patterns. Someone may commit a single act of adultery, repent, and be forgiven by God. Then there is the habitual adulterer, who has no intention of stopping his adultery. Occasionally he might be sorry, *if* he is caught, but he has no remorse for the act itself. He is labeled an adulterer because it is a perpetual practice, habit, or way of life for him. He may also justify and make excuses for his actions: "My wife doesn't understand me" and so on. There is no repentance and therefore no mercy because he does not believe he requires it.

Anger had become a habitual way of life for me. As long as I made excuses or laid blame, I rejected mercy by saying I was right to act and behave that way because of _____. Then I would insert the appropriate excuse for the incident. This Scripture jerked my eyes open. Written by Paul to the Galatian believers, he was repeating something he had already told them—because it was important. Those who continued in habitual lifestyles of sin would not inherit the kingdom of God.

Now at this point we could get into a big theological discussion as to exactly what all the "kingdom of God" entails. Does it mean you go to heaven but have to live in the suburbs outside the kingdom? Or is the kingdom not really heaven but something different? Or does it mean the worst-case scenario—that you end up in hell? Though I lack a doctorate in theology, I am smart enough to realize that none of these are good options if we are being warned against them.

I had, at this point, been released from the spiritual weight of guilt and sin, but there still remained the habit issue. Each of us remembers being born again, experiencing the liberty and newness of life, then encountering numerous situations in which the mettle of our salvation experience was tested. We were given multiple opportunities to choose obedience and life when disobedience and death looked (for the moment) more appealing. Now my eyes were open, and I had some constructive choices to make. It was time to deny myself and take up my cross.

TAKE UP YOUR CROSS

The first step for me was releasing every person I had withheld forgiveness from. We will cover this process in-depth in a later chapter. The second step, confession, was a little more difficult for me.

I felt the Spirit leading me, and I confessed what had almost happened with Addison to my husband when he returned home that day. At first I protested, "But it didn't happen, so why does John have to hear about this?"

> *Our hearts are hotbeds for good or bad seed.*

I believe the reason this was necessary was threefold. First, the kingdom does not operate on merely natural principles. Remember, Jesus told the Pharisees that whoever looks at a woman with lust had committed adultery with her in his heart. Heart issues are of utmost importance in the kingdom. Our hearts are hotbeds for good or bad seed. It hadn't happened in the physical realm in my case, but it had occurred in my heart. The shame and horror of it had already played themselves out in living color.

And though I was forgiven when I confessed my sin to the Father in the name of Jesus, look what the book of James tells us: "Therefore confess your sins to each other and pray for each other so that you may be healed. The prayer of a righteous man is powerful and effective" (James 5:16 NIV).

By humbling myself through confessing my sin and praying with my husband, I positioned myself for a healing in this area. I had already been forgiven when I repented and confessed my sin to God, but healing flowed into the dark recesses of my heart when I brought my sin into the open. Confession sheds light on areas of sin and shame, and in this atmosphere of light prayer brings healing and restoration.

> *With revealed truth came responsibility to truth.*

The third reason it was good to bring this to John was that it gave me a level of accountability. With revealed truth came responsibility to truth. I now knew the truth, but would I choose to live by truth? John was the ideal person for me to be accountable to, even though he might not have been the most sympathetic. I probably could have called a friend who was also a mother of multiple preschoolers and told her what almost happened, and she might have had sympathy and said something like, "Don't worry about it . . . I almost slammed my kid against the wall last week. You didn't actually do it." But the Word tells us: "Faithful are the wounds of a friend" (Prov. 27:6 NKJV).

I didn't need sympathy, I needed a faithful spanking from a friend. I needed someone to wound me with the truth. John fit the bill perfectly, yet he graciously did not condemn me. He could see how repentant and broken I was about the whole issue. We prayed together, and I felt a load of shame lift off my shoulders. But there remained the issue of habits to deal with.

The next day would begin my proving ground. As you probably have gathered, I have a tendency to be strong-willed. Now I had a choice. I could try to break the cycle of rage in my own strength and more than likely fail, or I could humble and deny myself, take up my cross, and acknowledge my utter dependency on God. This meant delving into the treasury of His Word and buffeting myself like a boxer in training with the truths I found there.

"BE QUICK TO LISTEN . . ."

I began by planting Scriptures that would bring forth a harvest of righteousness in my life. One of my favorites was found again in the book of James: "My dear brothers, take note of this: Everyone should be

> How do you break a habit? The same way you developed it.

quick to listen, slow to speak and slow to become angry" (1:19 NIV). He prefaced his address to his Christian brothers with the admonition to take note of what he was going to say. Then he made it all-inclusive: Everyone! That includes leaders, parents, children, bosses, employees, and definitely postpartum mothers. No matter what the position, everyone is to be quick to listen to others, slow to speak, no matter how quickly something may pop into their head in response, and slow to become angry.

I was modeling the exact opposite of this behavior. I was quick to speak, slow to listen, and quick to wrath! I didn't have it right in a single area. I believe that is because these traits are interrelated.

If you slow down your response time by removing the pressure to exert your input quickly, you can really listen to what the other person is saying. Often this prevents you from overheating, the other person from moving to the defensive, and it all works out better.

This led to enlisting God's help in my mouth department. Like David my prayer became: "Set a guard over my mouth, O LORD; keep watch over the door of my lips" (Ps. 141:3 NIV).

A guard watches what comes in and what goes out. David eloquently compared our lips to doors because they can be opened or shut. He pleaded that a guard be posted over his mouth so the wrong words might not escape and do damage. The Holy Spirit will take the Scriptures you have hidden in your heart and bring them to your remembrance just when you are about to let harmful words escape.

Scientific studies have proved that it takes a total of twenty-one days to break a habit. This is based on how long it takes for amputees to lose the ghost image of a lost limb. After three weeks they will no longer try to catch or support themselves with the phantom appendage.

Remember, habits are strong. They are responses we enact without thinking, just as we use our limbs without

> With God all things are possible.

thinking. Rage had become a habit in my life. To think of navigating twenty-one days without an infraction seemed an impossibility. It might as well have been twenty-one years. Rage was that ingrained in me.

How do you break a habit? The same way you developed it. One incident at a time, five minutes at a time, one hour at a time, one day at a time. When I awoke the next morning I immediately humbled myself: "God, I need You today. Place an extremely ruthless and severe guard over my mouth. I don't want to sin against You. Help me today to be slow to speak, quick to listen, and slow to wrath."

I didn't think, *I've got to do this for twenty more days. Oh no! This is impossible . . . It's all too much!* I didn't allow it to overwhelm me even though it could have. Instead I took it one small bite at a time.

I am not telling you it was easy; it was not. But I am telling you that with God all things are possible. I have lived more than ten years in a state where rage no longer controls me . . . I control it.

The first two steps on the road to freedom are repentance and confession. The closing chapter of this book contains a twenty-one day journal and Scripture diary to help you walk that road with what God has begun in your heart.

Dear Heavenly Father,

Forgive me and wash me clean. I don't want to just repent of the fruit of my anger. I want the sword of Your Word to cut out the very root of anger in my life. As I read on, continue to open my eyes that I might see. I thank You for the conviction of Your Spirit which has drawn out the shadows of justification and blame. I embrace the light of Your truth and the freedom of forgiveness.

10 The Power of Confession

As I travel and speak, there are many precious women who share that they didn't even realize how angry they were until they heard me speak and saw themselves in the mirror of my life. They often weep and share how they cannot wait to go home, apologize, and begin their lives anew.

Perhaps you are feeling much the same way. You have caught a glimpse of yourself in my words and long for a new beginning. Do you believe it is by accident that you hold this book in your hands? No, I believe it is by divine purpose. When we encounter another believer whose life has been touched in an area of our need, faith will rise and hope will spring anew. We step out on the water and with quaking hearts question, "Lord, is that You? God, is this something You could possibly do for me? Could You forgive me and wash me clean from all my sin and shame? Can I dare to dream You might completely transform my present rage to godly anger? Could this be an area where Your Holy Spirit could inhabit my life and You would be glorified by the way I handle conflict?"

To all of these questions and any others your trembling heart may ask, the heavenly Father answers, "Yes!"

We Have a Helper

I have been where you are. Though I have not seen your face and do not know your name, I do know we are not that different. Because the Bible tells us,

> No temptation has seized you except what is common to man. And God is faithful; he will not let you be tempted beyond what you can bear. But when you are tempted, he will also provide a way out so that you can stand up under it. (1 Cor. 10:13 NIV)

There is no problem you will face that is uniquely yours. But Satan loves to isolate and accuse each of us. He whispers lies, such as "You are the only one who struggles with such things. You are

> *There is no problem you will face that is uniquely yours.*

alone with this . . . No one else is as hateful as you!" I know because, like you, I have heard this lie.

God is no respecter of persons. This means He does not play favorites when it comes to His promises and to His Word.

> Then Peter began to speak: "I now realize how true it is that God does not show favoritism but accepts men from every nation who fear him and do what is right." (Acts 10:34–35 NIV)

Our heavenly Father receives each and every child who comes before Him with a humble and obedient heart. Remember, it is not the prideful and self-righteous our Lord accepts but the broken and contrite. Nor is it the independent one or the know-it-all whom he hears. He hears those who come spent of themselves and tired of trying. To these weary, broken ones He invites: "If any of you lacks wisdom, he should ask God, who gives generously to all without finding fault, and it will be given to him" (James 1:5 NIV).

Acknowledging our lack of wisdom is an act of humility in itself. We must admit that we have tried everything possible in our own strength and yet have failed in our attempts. When we are tired of blaming others only to remain captive ourselves and are ready to let go of all the blame, then we can freely come before our heavenly Father, who is not looking at or for our faults and shortcomings. He looks past all our feeble attempts and searches the deep realms of our hearts.

WALK IN THE LIGHT

> But if we walk in the light, as he is in the light, we have fellowship with one another, and the blood of Jesus, his Son, purifies us from all sin. (1 John 1:7 NIV)

What does it mean to "walk in the light, as he is in the light"? In answer we must look at a preceding verse, 1 John 1:5: "God is light; in him there is no darkness at all." God not only walks in light, He is Light. This light does not emanate from any external covering but explodes forth from His very being. There is no darkness in any part of Him. This is a hard concept for us to even imagine let alone envision. Everything we see is shaded and shadowed in one manner or another. The only light sources we know of cause shadows. The apostle John was not referring to a light source that originates or shines outside or around us but to one that proceeds from us.

He was not referring to natural physical light but to the light of our spirit (though in heaven, as with Moses, it may actually be physically visible). We walk in the light in this present dark

> *God not only walks in light, He is Light.*

95

and shadowed world by walking in purity of heart. We remove areas of darkness in our lives by allowing the blood of Jesus to cleanse us. This restores and maintains our fellowship with other believers and with God. But, "If we claim to be without sin, we deceive ourselves and the truth is not in us" (1 John 1:8 NIV).

How do we claim to be without sin? Most of us do this without realizing it. Again, when we justify, blame, or make excuses for our behavior, we in essence claim to be faultless. It can be heard in our conversations: "I'm sorry. I know I should not have . . . but you make me so mad when you do that!" For most of us this line of reasoning is all too familiar. We have said this in some form since we were children. But this is not an apology by any means. Instead it is a way of placing blame. We have not taken responsibility nor are we sorry for our actions. We are merely saying, "I'm sorry, but you irritate me! It is your fault. You made me mad and therefore suffered due consequence. I had no choice in the matter. You pushed me beyond my level of control." First John 1:8 says that when we follow this pattern of claiming to be without sin we deceive ourselves and "the truth is not in us." It is one thing to have a knowledge of the truth and quite another to live it. The Pharisees were experts in the letter of the truth yet they lacked the spirit of it. Psalm 119:105 declares, "Your word is a lamp to my feet and a light for my path" (NIV). The Pharisees possessed great knowledge yet walked in darkness. Jesus called them whitewashed tombs filled with dead men's bones. They looked light on the outside, but inwardly they were filled with dark-

> *We remove areas of darkness in our lives by allowing the blood of Jesus to cleanse us.*

> *It is one thing to have a knowledge of the truth and quite another to live it.*

ness and the stench of death. They justified their greed and cruel use of God's Word by their positions and performance. They cloaked themselves in deception. But God is not looking for position or performance. He is not impressed by titles and the praise

> *He wants clean hands and a pure heart.*

of men. He wants clean hands and a pure heart. These come through humility, transparency, and honesty.

> If we confess our sins, he is faithful and just and will forgive us our
> sins and purify us from all unrighteousness. (1 John 1:9 NIV)

Jesus purifies those who confess. This refers again to walking in the light. Confession illuminates or brings to light an issue. To confess is to admit, tell, own up, acknowledge, concede, or unburden oneself. When we confess we unload the darkness, take responsibility, and accept our share of the fault. I have to admit there have been times I have even gone to God and made excuses. "God, I know I shouldn't have . . . but they make me so mad!" When I do this, I'm not asking for mercy or cleansing; I'm making excuses. I will leave His presence still feeling dirty and offended. Guilt and condemnation will shadow me and darkness will shroud my path.

But when we openly own up to not only our actions but also to our motives, we find ourselves cleansed from all unrighteousness. God forgives our sins and purifies us. Recently I bought my son Alexander a new shirt that he was excited about getting. Unfortunately the very first time he wore it he spilled something on it. He brought it home, held it up for my inspection, and then looked up to me with his big brown eyes and said, "Sorry, Mom."

No excuses, no blaming, just, "Sorry, Mom."

How could I be upset? I knew the shirt was something he was disappointed about staining.

"That's okay," I assured him. "I'll try to get the stain out."

He was so honest about the whole thing and his manner so winsome, I immediately started yet another load of laundry. (With four boys I can always find a load of wash to do somewhere.) I took special care to pretreat his shirt, and since he had shown me the stain right away I was able to get it out completely, without even a trace remaining. He knew he was already forgiven, but now he felt restored. He would not have to look down at his garment and see any traces of the stain.

I believe this illustrates what happens when we truly confess. We are forgiven, pretreated with the blood of Jesus, and every bit of stain is removed from our life. God is always willing and able to forgive us, but when we do not confess in accordance with the word of truth that is in us, we continue to be stained with unrighteousness. We have His promise, though, that if we confess, He is faithful and just to first forgive and then to purify us of all unrighteousness. Blaming and justifying are symptoms of self-righteousness in a believer's life.

> *If we confess, He is faithful and just to first forgive and then to purify us of all unrighteousness.*

God's Word tells us there is no one righteous, no not one! Therefore, "If we claim we have not sinned, we make him out to be a liar and his word has no place in our lives" (1 John 1:10 NIV).

If we claim that we are sinless we contradict God's Word: "For all have sinned and fall short of the glory of God" (Rom. 3:23 NIV). When we excuse as weakness what God calls sin we call Him a liar. When we say it is impossible to obey His Word, which says there is no temptation we do not have the ability in Christ to overcome, we contradict Him and make Him out to be a liar.

It is imperative that we just open up before Him and expose the good, the bad, and the ugly. There is no secret sin or dark motive in our hearts that He is not already acquainted with. He knows us better than we know ourselves. *Confession therefore is not a matter of informing God but of denying ourselves and admitting to or agreeing with God's Word of truth.*

Often this can be painful, as it was for me when I glimpsed for the first time the absolute wretchedness of the full spectrum of my rage. Perhaps even now you are experiencing similar emotions. You're even afraid you will not be able to change. The truth is, more than likely you cannot. Without the Word of God and the intervention of God most of us have an extremely difficult time chang-

> *It is imperative that we just open up before Him and expose the good, the bad, and the ugly.*

ing our habits. You have already tried it on your own and failed; now it is time to allow God to have His way. It is important you that do not measure what *God* can do in the future by what *you* have done in the past. God is not limited by or confined to our failings.

BROKEN AND IRRESISTIBLE

Scripture says, "God opposes the proud but gives grace to the humble" (James 4:6 NIV). I don't know anyone who would enjoy the opposition of the King of heaven and earth. Another translation tells us that God resists the proud. I don't know about you, but I don't want God resisting or opposing me. I want to be broken and irresistible to God. I cannot make it without His help and assistance. In order for this to happen, I must humble myself through repentance, openly confess not only my actions but also my motives, thus presenting any darkness in my heart, then embrace His forgiveness and receive His cleansing and purifying process.

"Submit yourselves, then, to God. Resist the devil, and he will flee from you" (James 4:7 NIV). After the process of submitting to

God we can resist the devil and he *will* flee. After submitting our hearts, our pasts, and our mistakes to God, it is time to resist the devil. Because we are no longer justifying our rage or blaming others, we no longer stand in our own righteousness but in God's. This moves us from the realm of self-righteousness and the dominion of what we have done or what was done to us. We now step into the domain of light where righteousness is based on what was done *for* us. When we humble ourselves we are stripped of our filthy rags of self-righteousness and clothed in the garments of the righteousness of Christ and the authority it provides.

It will be necessary to resist the devil when he comes with his lies and accusations. He will not stop accusing you just because you have repented and confessed. He will continue to bring up your past failings. Often we are tempted to wallow in his accusations for a little while. In my case, before embracing God's mercy by truly denying myself and confessing my sin I would attempt to punish myself.

This took many forms but here I will share a few. I would punish myself by withholding forgiveness. You may be wondering how I could possibly be able to accomplish such a feat when Jesus freely forgives. Well, I would not allow myself to confess what I had done until I felt sufficiently guilty. Because of the delay, shame and condemnation crept in, replacing the initial conviction I experienced. When I finally did confess, I found it was not really a true confession but more of an apology . . . and there is a difference.

CONFESSION VS. APOLOGY

Did you notice when I described what it meant to confess earlier in this chapter, there was no mention of apologizing? There is a vast difference in their root meanings. The definition of *apology* includes: "excuse, defense, justification, and explanation."

Remember, apologetics is the defense of a belief. Therefore, a classic example of apology is, "I'm sorry, but you made me mad." Or "I'm sorry, but I can't help it." Or "I'm sorry, but it's not my fault." The condemnation and shame would be so heavy on me that I felt better about apologizing than about confessing. Confession is "no holds barred" while apologies are conditional.

You may find this surprising, but the term *apology* or *apologize* does not even appear in the

> ～ *Confession is "no holds barred" while apologies are conditional.*

Bible. Not only did I apologize to God, but I also apologized to others. Confessions pave the way to forgiveness because they acknowledge the need for it; apologies do not.

The longer we delay confession to God the deeper the imprint of guilt on our souls. It is not unlike the stain on my son's shirt. What if he had been ashamed and instead of bringing the soiled shirt to me right away he had hidden it under his bed or casually thrown it into the laundry hamper? The stain would have had more of an opportunity to set into the fibers of the material and would have been harder to remove. And what would his actions have said to me? If he had hid it from me I would have thought he was afraid of my reaction and viewed me as unfair. If he had thrown it into the hamper, neglecting to bring it to my attention, I might have missed the spot altogether in the laundry pretreating process and again there would have been a greater chance for a stain. By bringing it to me as soon as possible, he showed me he believed that I would not overreact and I would do whatever was within my power to remove it. God wants us to approach Him with the same heart.

But without faith it is impossible to please Him, for he who comes to God must believe that He is, and that He is a rewarder of those who diligently seek Him. (Heb. 11:6 NKJV)

I took pleasure in the fact that he had brought it to me right away. Faith is not only believing God is, but also that He is good and fair and rewards those who are diligent in their pursuit of Him. I don't want you to limit the meaning of *diligence* as applying only to work. It encompasses far more. It includes constancy, patience, application, industry, and zeal. Someone who consistently turns to God is an example of diligence.

> *Faith is not only believing God is, but also that He is good and fair and rewards those who are diligent in their pursuit of Him.*

SELF-PUNISHMENT

Another way I would punish myself was to repeatedly rehearse my failures while berating myself with them. "How could I have been so stupid!" "Boy, Lisa, you just keep doing this over and over again." "No one else is as bad as you. No one else fights the battles you do. Everyone else is a better, stronger Christian than you are!" By allowing these nagging, accusing conversations airtime in my mind, I hoped to prevent further infractions by shaming myself into a new behavior pattern. This served the purpose of increasing sin-consciousness in my life until I was overwhelmed by it. I imagined the accusing voices were God's thoughts toward me. When I came before Him in prayer, I found the choir of accusations drowning out the still, small voice.

I would apologize to God and my husband again and again, and yet as the words came out of my mouth I felt doomed to repeat my mistakes. But when I confessed and renounced for the first time, I saw light at the end of my dark tunnel. It was then I realized the way out of any dark cave or tunnel is found not by looking at the darkness but by moving toward the light. Confession, not apology, moves us toward the light.

I also punished myself by allowing this guilt into my relationships with my husband and God. I imagined they really hadn't forgiven me. After all, how could they forgive me when I had yet to forgive myself? This caused me to put up a mental wall and be guarded. God does not say, "Punish yourself, beat yourself up, and when you have paid the price come to Me." No. He wants us to be angry and sin not. He does not want the sun to go down on our wrath toward others or toward ourselves.

Peter was addressing the very Jews who had called for the crucifixion of his Lord in Acts 3:19: "Repent, then, and turn to God, so that your sins may be wiped out, that times of refreshing may come from the Lord" (NIV).

In this Scripture Peter was addressing a large crowd of people, but his message also has personal application to our lives. When we repent (not apologize) our sins are wiped out, and we experience a "refreshing" in our relationship with the Lord. We are showered and washed of our filth. There is nothing more refreshing than a thorough washing.

We have covered our confessions with God; now let's turn to our confessions to men.

Heavenly Father,

I come to You in the name of Jesus. Thank You for opening my eyes. No longer will I merely apologize . . . I will confess my role and part. I will receive Your cleansing from every stain. I thank You that not even a trace will remain. Now, Lord, I ask for Your refreshing. Blow the wind of Your Spirit on the dry bones of my life. Wash me in the water of Your Word.

11   *Stopping It Before It Gets Out of Hand*

Wouldn't it be nice if we somehow could avoid any type of intense conflict in the first place? This would eliminate or greatly reduce the amount of time we spend confessing the sins of our mouth. If we find the source of contention then we can possibly avoid its escalation in our lives.

INNER CONFLICT

James asked, "What causes fights and quarrels among you? Don't they come from your desires that battle within you?" (James 4:1 NIV). Oh no! This appears to be another internal affair. There appears to be yet another battle of desires being waged within us.

He continued, "You want something but don't get it. You kill and covet, but you cannot have what you want. You quarrel and fight. You do not have, because you do not ask God" (4:2 NIV). Well, maybe this isn't a new battle. Maybe it's just a continuation of symptoms from the other. This sounds awfully reminiscent of Cain and Abel. This cannot help but happen when we make other people our source of provision. If they are our source then they also become our withholders. If we believe man provides promotion and security then we will become fearful and angry if we are not in control. James was telling his listeners the reason they were quarrelling and fighting among themselves when they instead needed to lift their eyes to heaven and seek God's wisdom.

"When you ask, you do not receive, because you ask with wrong motives, that you may spend what you get on your pleasures," James stated (4:3 NIV). This used to confuse me. Was James contradicting himself here? No, he was not admonishing them to "ask God" and then telling them it is useless to ask God. So what was he saying? I believe in explanation we could use the following paraphrase:

> Do you know why you're always in strife? It is because of what is going on inside you! Look at your motives! Whenever you don't get what you want, you throw a fit and become destructive. You continue to lust for the possessions and positions of others. You're so out of control, you'd even kill to get your way! You cannot have what you want! God won't allow it, and you need to ask Him why. But instead you rage at and blame those around you. Whenever you ask for things with these motives you will not receive because God knows they will be wasted on your own pleasures.

I have had to put this into practice with my children. When they were young, sometimes my precious, beautiful angels would hit, call names, or throw fits to get their way (not unlike their mother). In the heat and intensity of a battle with a two-year-old, it would often appear easier for all involved to just let him have his way. Let him win this battle in hopes you might later win the war. Well, you might—but only after greater difficulty and with much more heartache than the initial confrontation presented. Rewarding bad behavior will always come back to bite you in the end. You ultimately are not doing the child a favor but a disservice. God is our heavenly Father, and He is the wisest of all parents. He knows when some desired *thing* will jeopardize our character.

I must confess that there have been times when I've found myself guilty of throwing a tantrum to get my way. I whined and complained,

"God, how come they have this and I don't?" evidencing my covetousness, or I'd stomp my foot and demand this or that. Other times it was interpersonal, "God, You know I'm right and they're wrong! Tell them or show them I'm right!" This was especially convenient in disagreements with my husband or other Christians. I imagined God interrupting their devotions to tell

> ✒ *Rewarding bad behavior will always come back to bite you in the end.*

them how right I was. Of course, these selfish and self-serving prayers were never serviced. Yet I found as I matured and dared to abandon myself and others into the hands of God, His righteousness, not mine, prevailed. I was usually granted the unique opportunity to glimpse myself from another perspective and to discover that the motives I thought were so pure in fact were not. Remember, you can be right and yet at the same time be wrong.

There are other reasons for unanswered prayers, one of which is unresolved conflict.

Unresolved Conflict

> Therefore, if you are offering your gift at the altar and there remember that your brother has something against you, leave your gift there in front of the altar. First go and be reconciled to your brother; then come and offer your gift. (Matt. 5:23–24 NIV)

When the temple was still intact, one would come before the altar to present his gift. It was a time of reflection and introspection. The gift was an unblemished covering for the iniquity in his life. Likewise we come before the Father in prayer, readying our hearts in order to present a sacrifice of praise. As we search the recesses of our soul, if iniquity is found it is to be confessed; but if we remember a brother who holds something against us, God tells us to stop the process, leave the gift, and first go to him and be reconciled.

Sometimes resolving conflict is easier said than done. When the conflict is between Christians we at least have the same frame of reference or standard for resolving issues. But sometimes those around us will refuse to be reconciled. Then what do we do? I had this happen once with a fellow Christian. I had inadvertently offended a friend and sensed there was a breach between us. I searched my heart and went to her. I asked if there was anything I had done to hurt or offend her. I volunteered the fact

> *We come before the Father in prayer, readying our hearts in order to present a sacrifice of praise.*

that I realized how I could often be offensive without my knowledge and assured her I did not want to stay that way. She told me I had done nothing, yet the measured distance still remained. I bought her a gift and left a note, again asking for forgiveness. I received no response. I went again in person. She assured me that no, there was nothing wrong, but still the distance remained. Finally I went to a mutual friend and asked her if she knew what I had done to offend this person. She did not. I poured out the whole story to her in an attempt to make sense of it. Finally, after listening to the whole thing, she said, "Lisa, have you asked her to forgive you?"

"Yes," I assured her.

"Have you reached out?"

"Yes, repeatedly," I said.

"If you've done all this and she still won't receive you, you have to let it go."

Her words set me free. I realized that I had obeyed Romans 12:18: "If it is possible, as far as it depends on you, live at peace with everyone" (NIV). I felt so guilty and at a loss because I wasn't even sure what my transgression was. The truth is, it is altogether possible that she no longer enjoyed our friendship, or the seasons in our lives had changed. I have watched some friends float in and out of my life as God has done a work in me or in them.

Our responsibility is to pray for reconciliation and ask God what role we are to play in the process. If we go to the person we wish to be

> ◁◯ *Our responsibility is to pray for reconciliation and ask God what role we are to play in the process.*

reconciled with in humility and love and are still rejected, sometimes it is because they are not yet ready to respond. No one likes to feel rejected. It hurts, but you are never a failure if you obey God's Word.

What if it is not a brother you are in conflict with but an adversary? God gives us advice in this area as well.

> Settle matters quickly with your adversary who is taking you to court. Do it while you are still with him on the way, or he may hand you over to the judge, and the judge may hand you over to the officer, and you may be thrown into prison. I tell you the truth, you will not get out until you have paid the last penny. (Matt. 5:25–26 NIV)

This adversary is so serious he will take you to court. I can almost envision the scene: a heated argument takes place that appears impossible to settle. Each side is firmly planted on their side of the fence. Finally one of them has had enough and decides he will sue. He snatches the arm of the other fellow and cries, "All right, this will be decided in court!" Before he can think, the other fellow is being propelled through the busy marketplace toward the judicial building in haste. He must think quickly. Does he want to go through the expense and embarrassment of court proceedings? Or would it be better to settle out of court and save himself all that trouble and expense? It is *always* better to settle out of court! So on the way he begins to negotiate a settlement. As one translation reads, "Agree with your adversary."

Jesus encourages us to come to a place of agreement before we are ever brought before the judge.

What works with an enemy will certainly work with a friend or husband. Being so mouthy for so long made this one very difficult for me. Actually my mouth was an outward manifestation of my inward condition of pride. There was a time of conflict in my life with a loved one and it went perpetually back and forth. This person would state a case . . . I'd state mine. It went back and forth like a tennis match with no hope of ending. We enlisted the help of a Christian counselor. After one night I was emotionally drained and thinking even counseling wouldn't help. All we had done was bring up the past and hurt each other again with it. John and I were driving home feeling hopeless when it hit me! *Hey, it really doesn't matter who is right. I am not going to defend myself or my position any longer. I think I'm right and I'm trying to make this person agree that I am. It is never going to happen. But I love this person and, right or wrong, I have hurt this relationship, so I need to do whatever I can to accomplish reconciliation.*

I went to sleep that night hopeful for the first time in years that God might have His way in our lives. The next day when we met again with the counselor I began by saying, "I just want you to know, I'm sorry for everything."

At first it didn't make a difference in this other person, but it made an immediate difference in me. I think the counselor was wondering what was going on with me because of the radical change from the night before. My friend brought up another incident for my inspection.

"I'm sorry," I said. I offered no excuses or justification, just "I'm sorry." Another incident came up, and again, "I'm sorry" was my reply. In just a short span of time the storm between us calmed. We hugged and looked forward to spending time together the following day.

God will be faithful to His Word when you submit to it and walk in it. It may not happen immediately, but it will happen. Even if someone else's heart still rages against you, He will keep you in perfect peace.

This is often so difficult for us, especially if we have a history of an issue with anger. The last thing we want to do in our own person is surrender. We want to fight to the finish. I was always under the mistaken impression that I was winning something when I threw the last word in edgewise. I thought whoever got in the most punches won. But I was wrong. We never win when we don't control our mouths, and controlling our mouths is a major key.

> ✎ God will be faithful to His Word when you submit to it and walk in it.

THE POWER OF THE TONGUE

We all stumble in many ways. If anyone is never at fault in what he says, he is a perfect man, able to keep his whole body in check. (James 3:2 NIV)

Here is where the ability to verbalize our thoughts has its disadvantages. What I say is definitely an area of constant challenge for me. I am a far cry from a perfect woman, with my body tightly in check. The good news is, by God's grace I have come a long way. Instead of skipping these verses as I used to, I use them like free weights. James goes on to illustrate in great detail the importance of taming your tongue:

When we put bits into the mouths of horses to make them obey us, we can turn the whole animal. Or take ships as an example. Although they are so large and are driven by strong winds, they are steered by a very small rudder wherever the pilot wants to go. Likewise the tongue is a small part of the body, but it makes great boasts. Consider what a great forest is set on fire by a small spark. (James 3:3–5 NIV)

He gives us some major visuals here. First there is the horse, who is much larger and stronger than a man, yet it can be turned or stopped in its tracks by the bit in its mouth. (I've often thought this might be a wonderful invention for human use as well.) Next we see the massive ship, driven through high seas yet directed by a very small rudder under the control of the pilot. Then we have the tongue. Again, it is small in comparison yet directs the course of our lives. It is like the small spark capable of destroying a great forest of wood.

> The tongue also is a fire, a world of evil among the parts of the body. It corrupts the whole person, sets the whole course of his life on fire, and is itself set on fire by hell. (James 3:6 NIV)

James directly correlated the tongue with fire and called it a world of evil in reference to the parts of the body. It has the potential to defile your whole person and send you down the path of destruction. It also holds the power to remove you from the kingdom of darkness and transport you to the kingdom of light.

> If you confess *with your mouth*, "Jesus is Lord," and believe in your heart that God raised him from the dead, you will be saved. For it is with your heart that you believe and are justified, and it is *with your mouth* that you confess and are saved. (Rom. 10:9–10 NIV, emphasis added)

The same thing that gets us into trouble can get us out of it: "The tongue has the power of life and death, and those who love it will eat its fruit" (Prov. 18:21 NIV). We are patterned after our heavenly Father, who uses His words to create and give life. This means we must choose to bless others with our words rather than curse them. We are called to be perfect as He is perfect. He is not requiring a physical perfection. The key is found in our speech. By bridling our tongue we control our whole being and may bring it under subjection to His Word of Truth.

"Who is wise and under-standing among you? Let him show it by his good life,

> *By bridling our tongue we control our whole being.*

by deeds done in the humility that comes from wisdom," James notes (3:13 NIV). It takes humility to be quiet when you really want to defend yourself. It takes humility to return a kindness for a treacher-ous act. Your life will follow your mouth. It is not usually the public things but rather the private things that get us into trouble. There is truly no such thing as a secret. Does this mean we should never talk and live in constant fear? No, we are admonished to

> Speak and act as those who are going to be judged by the law that gives freedom, because judgment without mercy will be shown to anyone who has not been merciful. Mercy triumphs over judgment! (James 2:12–13 NIV)

Here we have that measure principle again—the measure we use on others is the measure that will be used on us. This is the order of the law that gives freedom. People who execute judgment without mercy reap judgment without mercy. Most of us are not members of the judicial system, yet every day we participate in it to one degree or another. It is found in our actions and our speech.

> *People who execute judgment without mercy reap judgment without mercy.*

James warned, "But if you harbor bitter envy and self-ish ambition in your hearts, do not boast about it or deny the truth" (James 3:14 NIV).

When these things are hidden in our hearts, it is difficult to speak and act graciously. They will always manage to cloud our actions and color our conversations. Unresolved offenses in our lives become a filter through which we process everything. If it is jealousy, you will find it difficult to rejoice with others. If it is selfish ambitions, you will look at everything in terms of how it benefits you.

Jesus used suppertime at a Pharisee's house to drive home the illustration of how our words can defile us. The religious leaders were up in arms because the disciples of Jesus had not washed in the tradition of the elders. They had neglected to wash their hands before eating! (Well, in my house we think this is a good and necessary tradition. Who knows what the hands of four boys could touch during a day. . . .) Jerusalem, a hub of multiple cultures, animals, flies, and limited sanitation was not known for its cleanliness. It was that was not what it is today. So it was important to clean up before a meal. But Jesus contrasted this health-conscious tradition with an even more important one: "What goes into a man's mouth does not make him 'unclean,' but what comes out of his mouth, that is what makes him 'unclean'" (Matt. 15:11 NIV).

Dirty hands make for dirty food, but this was not the type of uncleanliness that would ultimately kill them. This rebuke greatly offended the Pharisees. They were experts in the outward appearance of cleanliness. Later in private Jesus interpreted it for His disciples: "Don't you see that whatever enters the mouth goes into the stomach and then out of the body? But the things that come out of the mouth come from the heart, and these make a man 'unclean.'" (Matt. 15:17–18 NIV).

HEART ISSUES

There we have it again. Out of the abundance of the heart the mouth will eventually speak. At times I have feared my own was a brood of vipers. I was afraid to open my mouth for fear that a snake of lethal words might pop out.

For out of the heart come evil thoughts, murder, adultery, sexual immorality, theft, false testimony, slander. These are what make a man "unclean"; but eating with unwashed hands does not make him "unclean." (Matt. 15:19–20 NIV)

Here we find a list of evil thoughts. Jesus lists murder and adultery. Isn't it interesting that both of these take place first in the heart? Jesus said that if you hate your brother, you're a murderer; and if anyone looks at a woman with lust he has already committed adultery with her in his heart.

Therefore it is the heart issues that will either produce or prevent fights. Stopping things before they get out of hand has more to do with what is happening inside than outside. Venturing into contentions is like navigating the crossing of a river. You never know just how fast or treacherous the current is until you're out in the middle of it, and at that point you are committed to the course. So often I can remember the turning point of a conversation when it went from good to bad or from bad to good. I could almost hear the Holy Spirit warn me, "Stay calm, lower your voice, answer gently. Don't say what you want to say, but listen to My still, small voice and speak My words instead." Sometimes I am obedient and listen . . . other times I just try to sneak in one more comment before obeying and find out just how costly my foolishness is. Proverbs 15:1 instructs us: "A gentle answer turns away wrath, but a harsh word stirs up anger" (NIV).

The Secret to Being Heard

I have found the secret to being heard. It really is quite simple: If you want to be heard, say it the way you would want to hear it. My children, my husband, my employees, my dog, in fact everyone actually listens more closely the quieter and calmer I am. I know I prefer to be spoken to in a gentle, respectful tone. I can hear so much better when I am not being yelled at. It is not the volume level or the repetition of words that grabs the attention, respect, and commitment of others. It is the weight of what we speak and the tone in which it is delivered. No one takes a person who is throwing a hissy fit seriously. Oh, they may get their way for the moment, but it will cost them later. We throw fits and raise our voices for a number of reasons. Here are a few:

> ✒ *If you want to be heard, say it the way you would want to hear it.*

1. We are afraid we are not being heard.

2. Yelling has produced results (getting our way) in the past.

3. We want to intimidate or control others.

4. It is what we lived as a child.

5. We are still angry over an unresolved issue.

6. It's a bad habit.

Most of these reasons are rooted in fear. God has not given us a spirit of fear but of power, love, and soundness of mind. We will yell and throw fits when we feel powerless. We will seek to intimidate and control others when we are self-serving. We will revert to our past when perfected love has yet to cast out fear. We overreact whenever we are bearing today the weight of yesterday's issues. We will continue in our bad habits if we have not renewed our minds to the truths of God's Word. We will always yield to fear's tactics when we fail to relinquish control to God and instead

> ✒ *We will continue in our bad habits if we have not renewed our minds to the truths of God's Word.*

attempt to maintain it ourselves. I found out a long time ago that no matter how things appear, I am not in control of them. I can control myself, but God is ultimately in control of everything. It is a manifestation of unbelief in our life when we refuse to surrender and submit to His truth and His will. Unbelief is at the root of any breach of trust we harbor in our relationship with God.

We fear that He won't deliver us or work out the situation in our best interest, so we wail like the children of Israel at the verge of their promised land, "What about our wives and children?" This translates to "What about me? What about mine?"

To stop things before they get out of hand, we must confess any and every area of unbelief and let go of these issues. We must commit ourselves to settling once and for all in our hearts that if we honor God by submitting to His Word, He will in turn honor His Word by transforming our situations. We must decide to rule our spirits and live according to His statutes. We must stop being foolish and embrace wisdom: "A fool gives full vent to his anger, but a wise man keeps himself under control" (Prov. 29:11 NIV).

> *I can control myself, but God is ultimately in control of everything.*

It is the fool who gives complete expression to his anger. Part of being angry without blowing it has a lot to do with maintaining your cool. To "vent" means to "blurt out, release, discharge, or verbalize." Think of those guards standing watch over your mouth. They are there to see to it that some words never escape your lips. The wise man has the same feelings and the same words clamoring to be given a voice, but he keeps himself; he is in control, not out of control.

> When words are many, sin is not absent, but he who holds his tongue is wise. The tongue of the righteous is choice silver, but the heart of the wicked is of little value. (Prov. 10:19–20 NIV)

A full venting usually includes an abundance of words of negative value. Note again, the wise woman could speak, wants to speak, but instead chooses to hold back her words. When a righteous person does speak, he

> ～ *Loose mouth = wicked heart;*
> *kept tongue = wise heart.*

has carefully chosen his words—words of value, not reckless, harmful ones. Notice again the parallel drawn between the tongue and the heart: loose mouth = wicked heart; kept tongue = wise heart. There is yet another step we can take.

CHOOSE TO OVERLOOK TRANSGRESSIONS

"The discretion of a man makes him slow to anger, and his glory is to overlook a transgression" (Prov. 19:11 NKJV). Again, being slow to anger makes you slow to speak and therefore slow to sin. The writer of Proverbs told us that it is our "glory" to overlook a transgression or an offense. It is to the honor, praise, eminence, and distinction of a Christian to overlook an offense. It is an example of our acting as Christ would.

> For to this you were called, because Christ also suffered for us, leaving us an example, that you should follow His steps: "Who committed no sin, nor was deceit found in His mouth"; who, when He was reviled, did not revile in return; when He suffered, He did not threaten, but committed Himself to Him who judges righteously. (1 Peter 2:21–23 NKJV)

It will only be possible to overlook insults, injuries, and threats if we have first committed ourselves to our Father, the righteous Judge. Often when my children are having a disagreement of sorts they will come to us to appeal to our sense of fairness. "He is not cleaning up enough," or "He has been on the computer too long." Their desire is, of course, first to have their cause heard and hopefully get their way, and second to see justice served. John and I will step in and officiate as best we can, but frequently they will not see our calls as fair. This leads to the dangerous situation of them taking the matter into their own little hands. I am not talking about conflict resolution; we encourage that. I am speaking of payment for perceived offenses. "Why did you hit your brother?" "Because he . . ." You've heard the list before. When we tell them to bring the problem to us instead of hitting, we will often hear, "But last time you didn't do anything." Which translates to "I decided I didn't like the way you handled it last time; therefore, I'm not taking a chance this time. I will handle it!"

John and I are the first to admit that we make mistakes as parents, but the good news is that God does not! He is a righteous and perfect Judge. His execution and sentencing may not be in the timing or manner that we would suggest, but His ways are perfect while ours are flawed. When we overlook an offense we are like trusting children who say, "Father, I know I can trust You with this one. It is

> ↘ *Examine your heart by the light of God's Word.*

too big and painful for me. I refuse to lash back; instead I lay it at Your feet and forgive." It is the gesture of royalty to do so. It is to imitate and shadow the Son of God in our earthly lives. Jesus told His disciples, "If [your brother] sins against you seven times in a day, and seven times comes back to you and says, 'I repent,' forgive him" (Luke 17:4 NIV).

There will be offenses in the life of each of us that we will need to overlook. To overlook something is to look above it, to choose to see things on a level higher than the committed offense. It is to extend grace and mercy where you would rather have exercised judgment.

In review here are some of our options in stopping things before they get out of hand:

1. Examine your heart by the light of God's Word.
2. Resolve existing conflict.
3. Settle matters by agreeing with your adversary.
4. Control your tongue.
5. Be merciful.
6. Be honest.
7. Answer gently.
8. Speak in the manner you'd want to be spoken to.
9. Choose your words wisely.
10. Overlook offenses and trust them to God.

In the next chapter we are going to discuss the physical consequences of unhealthy anger. Again, the importance of resolving a conflict in a healthy way cannot be overemphasized.

Heavenly Father,

I come to You now in the name of Jesus. I realize it is possible to avoid some conflicts. I choose to walk in the light of Your truth and as a child of the Most High. Create in me a clean heart that I might hear Your voice and not sin against You. I want to, whenever possible, live at peace with all men. I will place Your Word in my heart that I might not sin against You. Holy Spirit, help me to choose my words in a manner that honors God. Help me to let go and overlook some offenses. I realize that sometimes this will mean the small and insignificant and other times it will mean letting go of what is too painful to hold. Father, I choose to trust You. Forgive any areas in our relationship where unbelief has kept me from You. I renounce the hold of fear and choose to walk in power, love, and soundness of mind. Quicken these truths in my spirit until they become as much a habit as my rage was before. Thank You that You are the Author and Finisher of my faith.

12 Truth or Consequences: It Will Get Physical

With tensed shoulders, clenched teeth, and flashing eyes of steel, her face is lifted high upon a neck tilted and turned in arrogant detachment. This woman moves quickly and purposely through a crowd. Only aware of those around her to the extent they are aware of her, she is ready to push aside or chide anyone who gets in her way. At some level she is actually *looking* for conflict . . . it gives her purpose and the chance to release some of the pent-up tension she feels expanding inside. The longer it takes to release it, the more uncomfortable she will become and the more uncomfortable she will make others. She is angry in a crowd, at work, at church, in her car, at the store, in her home. She finds no haven from her anger.

As of yet she is not sure she wants a haven. Her rage makes her feel empowered, strong, and impenetrable. No one knows when or where she will blow up next. She keeps them guessing and leaves a trail of chaos in her wake . . . she likes it this way. When everything is out of control she is the only one in control. She alone knows what is really going on. She knows a secret: It doesn't really matter if everyone changes, if everything is perfect, if everything goes her way . . . she is still going to be angry. It is one thing to be angry and upset momentarily; it is quite another to live in a perpetual state of slow-burn rage, to live on the edge of the boiling point. At a moment's notice she can stoke the fire and allow it to boil over again. Employees, acquaintances, and loved ones have learned to avoid this at all cost and desperately try to please her. Wiser ones learn this will never happen and turn from her. She doesn't give them a thought. She doesn't let herself care—she is young and strong and will move on to other relationships.

There is another woman. Her shoulders are bent forward as though a shawl were wrapped tightly around her in which she hides. Her frightened eyes dart at unseen fears then return to the blank expression of one too long disappointed. Her neck is also bent forward, in support of a head hung heavy in shame. In contrast she is painfully aware of those around her. She imagines they look at her with contempt and speak of her in whispered tones of disdain; therefore, she cowers in their presence. But rarely do they really notice her. She is not a threat to them, at least not in the way she is to herself. She shuffles through her world of distrust and fear, feeling used and mistreated. Everyone else controls her life. Nothing is fair and she is a victim . . . and she is mad about it, but she hides it within the confines of herself. Everywhere she goes rejection follows her like a dark shadow. Others have tried to reach into her dim world to pull her out, but because they were less than perfect she scorned their attempts and remained in the familiarity of her lonely prison.

"I've been hurt again and again, and I'm not going to let them do it to me anymore," she mutters with resolve as she shuffles through life a magnet for the very abuse she fears.

Heart Attitudes

Though it may seem unlikely, both the angry strong woman and the beaten-down weak woman will one day find themselves in very similar situations. Both will more than likely be alone, even if they are married, because they do not possess the basic ingredients for real intimacy. The years go by and they may pass one another on the street and see reflected deep frown lines weighing down skin grayed before its time, clawed hands, backs bent under some unseen weight. You may ask, "Isn't this just the natural by-product of aging?"

Yes and no. The passage of years and the pull of gravity cannot

> ﹉ *Cheerful will always outlast beautiful.*

be avoided by any of us. But our responses to how those years are spent determine the quickness of our smile, the light in our eyes, and the softness of our edges. The attitudes of our hearts imprint themselves more than the illusion of cosmetics.

"A happy heart makes the face cheerful, but heartache crushes the spirit" (Prov. 15:13 NIV). Cheerful will always outlast beautiful. Beauty is fleeting, but a kind and gentle countenance will endure. You can have a cheerful face regardless of your age. Its glow will soften the effects of the passage of years. Your face can either be lined from repeated smiles or repeated frowns. You can choose the unconscious expression of your resting face, the one you revert to when no one is looking. This expression will reflect whatever you entertain in your times of inward conversation or the meditations of your heart. The opposite is true as well: "The north wind brings forth rain, and a backbiting tongue, an angry countenance" (Prov. 25:23 NASB).

Ugly words springing from a bitter heart yield an angry countenance as surely as the northern winds bring rain. Remember, Jesus told us that it is not what goes into a man but what comes out of a man that defiles him. When we allow our mouths to spew forth bitterness

> ﹉ *Habitual anger sows suspicion and fear where there should be trust; violence where there should be safety; and hostility where there should be intimacy.*

unchecked, it cannot help but show up on our faces.

If you foolishly embrace rage as a garment of strength or hide yourself in the shrouded past of unresolved issues, it will inevitably and eventually drain the very life from you. You will destroy the relationships around you, then turn inward and eventually self-destruct. This is true regardless of whether you inflict your anger on others or yourself.

Ungodly anger or rage causes you to push away and alienate the very ones you need and long to draw near. We all need an atmosphere of supportive relationships to flourish and grow throughout our lives. Habitual anger sows suspicion and fear where there should be trust; violence where there should be safety; and hostility where there should be intimacy.

A WOMAN'S NATURE

As women, our very nature and physical design are set up with nurture and tenderness in mind. We are not constructed with hard edges but gentle curves. We are initially created with a greater capacity for tenderness and compassion than men. We feel both love and pain deeper within our being. We are more empathetic than males and can be moved to tears over the pain, struggles, and losses of total strangers. When we are not allowed to express these emotions in a valid way, we run the risk of exploding either outwardly or inwardly.

When we go against our original design or purpose for creation, we actually war physically against our bodies. Women are created to be healthy and passionate, loving and compassionate. We violate the life-giving, strengthening, and supportive role in our lives when we are not. Women can fulfill this role whether they are married or single. I have a friend, Mary, who is always supportive and life-giving in her interactions with others. She speaks the truth in love, which means she speaks in a manner that can be heard. She is meek and gentle, yet strong. She is a focused servant of the Lord who lives to serve others. She is single yet daily practices the principles of a godly woman. If we lack these principles, they become glaringly apparent in our role as a helpmeet or a wife.

Here are two of my least favorite Scripture spankings. These were often quoted to me in my newlywed days: Better to live on a corner of the roof than share a house with a quarrelsome wife (Prov. 25:24 NIV). Or the other even *less* attractive version: Better to live in a desert than with a quarrelsome and ill-tempered wife (Prov. 21:19 NIV).

Life on the corner of a roof would mean being exposed to the extremes of all the elements. The roof provides no shelter from rain, snow, wind, or the harsh sun. Solomon was telling us it is better to live under these conditions than share the comfort and shelter of a house with a quarrelsome wife. There is more danger and harm to be found under the roof than on top of it. I used to argue with John that back then they used the roof as a type of alternative to the porch, but I found the reemphasis of this Scripture hard to explain away. Better to live in the desert or wilderness with the serpents and scorpions, not to mention the lack of vegetation or moisture as well as the exposure to the harsh elements, than with an angry, grumpy, and argumentative wife. This warring becomes wearing . . . not only on others but also on ourselves.

HEART HEALTH

"A cheerful heart is good medicine, but a crushed spirit dries up the bones" (Prov. 17:22 NIV). The Bible gives us amazing insight into the source of our health. Moisture is found in the marrow or center of the bones. This is where the immune system and the blood cells are fortified. Our life is in the blood, and our blood is fortified from the marrow in our bones. If the bones dry up, the very source of our life is compromised. This is confirmed again in Proverbs 14:29–30: "A patient man has great understanding, but a quick-tempered man displays folly. A heart at peace gives life to the body, but envy rots the bones" (NIV).

The Bible contrasts patience with a quick temper and peace with envy. Patience gives understanding, while a quick temper makes evident all the folly in one's life. A peaceful heart gives life to a body, while envy or ill will corrupts or rots your very bones. Isn't it amazing that some forms of cancer are treated by a bone marrow transplant? The health of our bone marrow is so crucial. But what could be more hidden? Encased in a hard shell of white and surrounded by muscles, organs, and miles of arteries, if there is a bone marrow problem it is often hard to detect without special tests. Bones are the structural support of our bodies. They are the frame by which we stand and without which we fall.

> A peaceful heart gives life to a body, while envy or ill will corrupts or rots your very bones.

The Bible confirms there is a real and ever-present relationship between the heart and health. I am not implying that everyone who is sick has an underlying heart problem. Certainly many get sick or die as young, innocent children. We live in a fallen world that is riddled by the curse of sickness and disease. What I am saying is that bitterness, unforgiveness, unresolved anger, and other heart issues directly affect your immune system. In his book *Make Anger Your Ally*, Neil Clark Warren reported that resentment is most frequently connected with punishing ailments, and frustration is a close second. He lists a sampling of these common ailments brought on by unresolved anger: headaches, stomach problems, colds, colitis, and hypertension.

Other studies have included afflictions ranging from types of arthritis, various respiratory ailments, skin disease, neck and back problems, to even cancer. I realize genetics and other environmental issues are factored into such things as lifestyle and diet, but the Bible has already declared for centuries what man is now finding to be true. Proverbs 3:5–8 is a wealth of wisdom concerning how we should live:

Trust in the Lord with all your heart and lean not on your own understanding; in all your ways acknowledge him, and he will make your paths straight. Do not be wise in your own eyes; fear the Lord and shun evil. This will bring health to your body and nourishment to your bones.

We have a promise here: If we live according to God's divine health plan, He says it brings health to our bodies and nourishment to our bones. Again God goes to the root of the issue. Not only does He provide health for the body; in addition He provides a future of health by nourishing our bones.

Eating disorders are often the result of unresolved anger issues. An individual has been deeply violated and wants to retreat and go

> ✍ *Eating disorders are often the result of unresolved anger issues.*

away. Often they have yet to realize a valid and healthy outlet for their anger so they punish themselves. This response to rejection becomes as tortured as anyone can imagine. We struggle against an enemy we cannot see with a voice we feel we cannot escape. I understand because I have lived that lie. (If this is an issue for you, my book *You Are Not What You Weigh* may be extremely helpful.)

If you are younger you may not have seen the physical effects of unchecked anger, but if you are older, chances are you have. Because it attacks the very basis of our immune system, it is important that we heed the warnings. Here is a Scripture with vivid imagery: "Whoever has no rule over his own spirit is like a city broken down, without walls" (Prov. 25:28 NKJV). And another version reads: "Like a city that is broken into and without walls is a man who has no control over his spirit" (NASB).

Unscalable Walls

In Bible times, walls were erected around cities as a source of protection. It was an obstacle that kept wild animals and enemies at bay. It is an unfamiliar concept for us, but these ancient cities were surrounded on all sides by unscalable walls. They stood as a warning to those on the outside: "You will not be allowed in until we know you are safe," as well as serving as a barrier of protection to those who lived within its walls. The gates to the city were closed each night and opened again in the morning. The inhabitants of the cities learned to trust in the walls and the gatekeepers for their protection from invaders and vandalism. These walls quarantined the ravages of sickness from other citizens. They even acted as barriers against wind, rain, and desert storms.

Now in light of this, imagine a city without walls, one that has been broken into and looted at will. Enemies and invaders come and go as they please. During the day the city is at the mercy of thieves, bandits, and enemy armies. There is no place to hide anything of value. Jackals and wild creatures pick through the ruins in the dark, making it a habitation of fear. Disease and infirmity slip in and out of its shadows. Who would want to live where there is no protection . . . where there is no shelter?

When we do not rule our spirit we inhabit just such a shadowy place. Our heart is no longer a haven or refuge of safety and peace, but it becomes a violated, looted city. We run off, an intruder on one side only to be invaded by another on the other side. Our protection is a constant concern but an impossible reality. Everything of real value has been carried off, and we have been reduced to a territorial security guard. The enemy comes and goes at will, trespassing both the inner and outer parameters of our life. Frustration becomes our daily bread, and sorrow and regret become our portion. After years of defending this undefendable city many of us will retreat to a shadowy corner of the rubble to hide in the ruins.

128

What if you have already realized that death and life are in the power of the tongue and you are not enjoying the fruit you are eating? You came out of the land of Egypt angry and cursing instead of blessing. Instead of finding the promised land, you have found yourself, your marriage, and your relationships in a wilderness of ruins. Every fortress you hoped to trust in has fallen down. The very temple of your physical body is suffering the ravages of years of unchecked anger and hateful remarks. What is left for you? How can the city of ruins be rebuilt? After repenting there is rebuilding. You have repented; now it is time to start the process of healing.

HEALING

"The tongue that brings healing is a tree of life, but a deceitful tongue crushes the spirit," according to Proverbs 15:4 (NIV). Replace your deceitful tongue with words that heal. Begin to speak words of life over your situations. Learn the Word of God and how it applies to your marriage, your work, your children, and your friendships. Begin to bless these areas of your life and refuse to curse them. Allow the Word of God to transform your soul, and you will reap the benefits physically.

The apostle John wrote to his friend Gaius, "Dear friend, I pray that you may enjoy good health and that all may go well with you, even as your soul is getting along well" (3 John 1:2 NIV).

Your health is affected by the well-being of your soul. There is no possible way to separate the two. They are intimately intertwined. Though words may not immediately inflict physical harm, the Bible compares them to a lethal weapon.

There is one who speaks rashly like the thrusts of a sword, but the tongue of the wise brings healing. (Prov. 12:18 NASB)

I can almost imagine an angry adversary attacking and assailing another. Loud and angry words are accompanied by painful stab wounds. There is a jab at the shoulder, another in the stomach, and one finds its mark in the upper arm. The victim is at first stunned then horrified as he slides down the wall until he is seated on the floor. He checks himself and sees that blood is staining his entire upper body. He feels faint and weak and closes his eyes for a moment. He finds himself enveloped in a black and fuzzy haze.

> ✎ Replace your deceitful tongue with words that heal.

Then he hears another voice. It is soft and gentle. He feels a warm and golden mist begin to creep into the darkness. The healing words are canceling out the very words spoken to wound him. He feels a gentle warmth calm the cold and fiery pain. Each pleasant word has a restorative effect on him. He awakes as if from a dream and finds himself healed and the wounding of the words soothed.

> Pleasant words are a honeycomb, sweet to the soul and healing to the bones. There is a way that seems right to a man, but in the end it leads to death. (Prov. 16:24–25 NIV)

Often it will seem right to openly air our grievances to allow our emotions to take center stage and be in full play. We think that by releasing these words we are freeing ourselves and informing others, but actually we are wounding ourselves as well as others. Without our knowledge our feet have turned from the path of life and to the way of death.

There is no way to avoid the connection between unhealthy anger and the quality of health we enjoy. It is imperative that you allow God to disengage you from any entanglement or entrapment that may have occurred as a result of past outbursts or injurious words. It matters not whether you spoke them or whether they were launched as missiles toward you by another. We must also include the insidious force of self-destructive words we so often use against ourselves. Examples of this would be, "No one really cares about me. In the end I will be alone and betrayed." "I'm ugly and fat. Why would anyone care?" These words wound and reinforce negative reactions and images in our lives. They construct a stronghold of pain through which each thought and action is processed. Let's pray:

> ✎ *There is no way to avoid the connection between unhealthy anger and the quality of health we enjoy.*

✎ *Dear Heavenly Father,*

I come to You in the name of Jesus. I realize my words at times have been reckless and injurious not only to others but to myself as well. Lord, may my tongue become an instrument of healing. Let my words be pleasant as a honeycomb and healing and restorative to the soul. Heal my very bones, and give me health and strength in the foundational core of my structure and my blood. Let any rottenness be replaced with life. Let any bitterness be removed from my life, and in turn use me as an instrument of healing in the lives of others. Allow me to bless those who have been cursed. Teach me to bless those who curse me. As I guard my mouth rebuild the walls of protection around my life. I will feed upon Your goodness, for "Your words were found, and I ate them, and Your word was to me the joy and rejoicing of my heart; for I am called by Your name, O LORD God of hosts" (Jer. 15:16 NKJV).

13 *Letting It Go*

At this point you've forgiven others, confessed your sins, and embraced the truth. Now comes the next step: You must release yourself. I know this is quite possibly harder than anything else, but it is a key element to your emotional, physical, and spiritual health. I often felt as though I should punish myself for my behavior before I would allow myself to be washed. I wanted the weight of guilt to bend me and shape me so I would never do it again. But guilt does not change us. I wanted to feel judgment, but instead I found God's mercy.

IN GOD'S MERCY

> Or do you show contempt for the riches of his kindness, tolerance and patience, not realizing that God's kindness leads you toward repentance? (Rom. 2:4 NIV)

It is the goodness and kindness of God that lead us to repentance. This goes against everything ingrained in us. We want to be punished when we fail. We want to pay; then we feel released from our guilt. God extends His mercy to cover what should be our judgment. We don't understand that concept. We are more geared to "an eye for an eye" and "a tooth for a tooth." We stand over the huddled figure of our shame and expect Jesus to proclaim judgment and reject us. The law and the accuser of the brethren always ask for judgment while the Spirit grants mercy. I want you to read anew this account of an obviously guilty woman and Jesus' response to her:

> The teachers of the law and the Pharisees brought in a woman caught in adultery. They made her stand before the group and said to Jesus, "Teacher, this woman was caught in the act of adultery. In the Law Moses commanded us to stone such women. Now what do you say?" They were using this question as a trap, in order to have a basis for accusing him. (John 8:3–6 NIV)

Notice that their real concern was not the pursuit of truth but to trap Jesus. I believe this is always the motive of the carnal nature as well as the accuser of the brethren's goal. He is not so much interested in discounting you as in degrading the work and validity of Christ. These religious leaders had no genuine concern for the salvation of this woman. I

> *It is the goodness and kindness of God that lead us to repentance.*

am here to tell you that the accusing voices you hear have no real concern for you, your family, or your quality of life. They only want to negate the work of Christ in your life and place you under the judgment of the law. Notice, at first Jesus did not even answer these religious leaders. He averted His eyes from their condemning and hateful gaze.

> Jesus bent down and started to write on the ground with his finger. When they kept on questioning him, he straightened up and said to them, "If any one of you is without sin, let him be the first to throw a stone at her." Again he stooped down and wrote on the ground. (John 8:6–8 NIV)

We do not know for certain what He penned in the dust. I have heard some leaders say He was writing the names of women whom these teachers and Pharisees had sinned with. Others have said He was writing the other commandments to remind them of their sins. For whatever reason, it is not recorded, but His response to them will stand for all time: "If any one of you is without sin, let him be the first to throw a stone at her." These men obviously felt extremely self-righteous as they dragged this sinful woman through the streets and displayed her for Jesus' judgment. Now the whole atmosphere changed. Their angry voices were silenced as their own hearts began to condemn them. They began to fear that this young Rabbi might start announcing the names for all to hear. Afraid to look Him in the eye, they departed one by one.

> At this, those who heard began to go away one at a time, the older ones first, until only Jesus was left, with the woman still standing there. (John 8:9 NIV)

Notice, it is the older ones who left first. I know I am much more merciful now that I am older than I ever was when I was young. Often the older have learned by experience not to judge too harshly or too quickly. They have more years of mistakes under their belts

> *Often the older have learned by experience not to judge too harshly or too quickly.*

and have mellowed in their zeal toward judgment. They have seen the ravages of hate and broken relationships. Now the woman was left alone before Jesus. Her accusers were gone and yet she stayed.

> Jesus straightened up and asked her, "Woman, where are they? Has no one condemned you?" "No one, sir," she said. "Then neither do I condemn you," Jesus declared. "Go now and leave your life of sin." (John 8:10–11 NIV)

When all the voices of accusation and condemnation were silenced, she waited before the Lord to hear what He might say. He questioned her as to the whereabouts of her accusers. She replied that there was no man left accusing her. Having been released from the accusation of man, Jesus then extended the mercy of God: "Neither do I condemn you." He released her from the weight of her sin and bondage, then admonished her to leave her life of sin. "Go and sin no more" is always preceded by mercy and forgiveness. Without these it is impossible for us to walk away from our lifestyle of rage and fury. Then Jesus returned to addressing the crowd:

> When Jesus spoke again to the people, he said, "I am the light of the world. Whoever follows me will never walk in darkness, but will have the light of life." (John 8:12 NIV)

THE LIGHT OF OUR WORLD

Jesus called Himself the Light of the World. Imagine what a bold statement this was. He then invited the people to follow Him and leave their paths of darkness to walk in the light of life. Apparently some of the Pharisees had hung around.

The Pharisees challenged Him, "Here you are, appearing as your own witness; your testimony is not valid" (John 8:13 NIV). They came to Him for judgment then told Him His testimony wasn't valid. Their protest shows that they did not come to Him for who He was but because of their jealous intent to expose Him.

> Jesus answered, "Even if I testify on my own behalf, my testimony is valid, for I know where I came from and where I am going. But you have no idea where I come from or where I am going." (John 8:14 NIV)

Jesus was the only Person alive who really did know where He came from and where He was going. He knew His purpose and destiny. He knew He was His Father's Son. The Pharisees who had gathered thought they were sons of Abraham and descendants of Moses, but really they were motivated by their father the devil. They did not know the standard of heaven, only the standard of men.

> You judge by human standards; I pass judgment on no one. But if I do judge, my decisions are right, because I am not alone. I stand with the Father, who sent me. (John 8:15–16 NIV)

He is letting them in on a secret: It was not His judgment but the Father's. In this case He had not accused or judged, but by forgiving He had released the woman from judgment. Mercy had set her free. Under the Law of Moses she should have ben put to death but Jesus understood that He would soon die as a sacrifice for her sin.

Even now He does not condemn. He looks at us and proclaims, "Go and sin no more." I'm sure the adulteress marveled at the revelation of forgiveness after being made so painfully aware of her sin and shame. The Pharisees and teachers of the law thought they had brought her to the

> ⟳ *"Go and sin no more."*

place of condemnation but found that they had not brought her before a judge but before Truth itself: "Then you will know the truth, and the truth will set you free" (John 8:32 NIV).

This woman had an encounter with the Truth immediately following a hopeless encounter with the law. What the law was powerless to do the Truth did. At His word she was set free in an instant from a life of sin and shame.

> Jesus replied, "I tell you the truth, everyone who sins is a slave to sin. Now a slave has no permanent place in the family, but a son

belongs to it forever. So if the Son sets you free, you will be free indeed." (John 8:34–36 NIV)

He turned her from a slave to a daughter and gave her a permanent place in the family. No longer would her identity be found in the arms of men; she had experienced the arms of love. Jesus had revealed Himself as forgiver of sin and liberator from darkness.

RELEASE YOURSELF

You may not be guilty of adultery or publicly exposed in the very act of a sin, but I am certain that you have heard the chorus of accusers. You have found yourself hopeless in a court of shame surrounded by those who were quick to point out your sin. Then the Son set you free . . . now you are free indeed. *Indeed* means "truly and of a certainty." You have confessed, now you must go from this place of sin, shame, and accusation, leave it behind, and sin no more. You must leave the court of man with all its condemnation and walk in the light of God. More often than not there will be no physical accusers involved in your battle. It will be waged in your mind, and the very voice that accuses you will be your own. But if God says you are not condemned and set free, you must walk in that truth.

We will never feel righteous because in and of ourselves there is no righteousness that could stand before a holy God. We are not the righteousness of God through our works or behavior but in Christ alone.

This righteousness from God comes through faith in Jesus Christ to all who believe. There is no difference, for all have sinned and fall short of the glory of God, and are justified freely by his grace through the redemption that came by Christ Jesus. (Rom. 3:22–24 NIV)

There is no sin so great that the blood of Jesus cannot cleanse it white as snow. He forgives our sin and removes the very stain of guilt so we have no need to revisit our past failures. We will always do best when we turn our eyes from our past failures and mistakes and lift our gaze to Him: "Forget the former things; do not dwell on the past" (Isa. 43:18 NIV).

This is the beauty and mystery of the new birth. Today is no longer bound to yesterday. We are free to step into a new manner of life, cleansed by mercy that is new every morning. Too often we are afraid we will be rejected—that our problem is too large or our sin too gross. Yet even now He is wooing you and calling you to lay aside all your defenses and simply believe.

> *There is no sin so great that the blood of Jesus cannot cleanse it white as snow.*

Do not be afraid; you will not suffer shame. Do not fear disgrace; you will not be humiliated. You will forget the shame of your youth and remember no more the reproach of your widowhood. (Isa. 54:4 NIV)

Jesus does not want us to fear humiliation and shame. He wants us to honor Him as holy, just, and true. Our anger even with ourselves can never work the righteousness of God in our lives. So what can continuing to withhold forgiveness from yourself accomplish? What benefit could that possibly hold? Nothing but self-loathing and destruction. Humbly release yourself and surrender now to His gentle mercy. We have His promise and can expect this to be His response to us: "You are forgiving and good, O Lord, abounding in love to all who call to you" (Ps. 86:5 NIV). It is time to call on Him now.

Heavenly Father,

I come to You in the name of Jesus. Forgive me for standing in the human court of shame and accusing myself by its standards. Lord, I embrace Your mercy. I will allow it to triumph over every area of judgment in my life. I leave this place of guilt and self-loathing and arise and go to sin no more. I could never punish myself enough to earn what You have so freely given with the sacrifice of Your life. Wash me anew in Your blood. I forgive myself for all the mistakes I have made. I confess my tendency toward self-righteousness; I turn from it and embrace Yours. This moment I start a new page of my life. Thank You, Father, for Your goodness and kindness, which have truly led me to repentance.

14 *Putting It into Practice: Maintaining Your Passion Without Losing Your Cool*

Remember this, my dear brothers! Everyone must be quick to listen, but slow to speak and slow to become angry. Man's anger does not achieve God's righteous purpose (James 1:19). What a profound statement. Man's anger does not achieve God's righteous purpose, yet so very often this is exactly our justification for our outrage. There has been an injustice of some sort or the other, and we want it righted. But anger will never be the solution to any righteous cause. God does not use the vehicle of *our* rage to serve His purposes. The truth is, we have tried to use our rage to serve our own purposes. We mistakenly thought it would protect, provide, guide, and empower us. Instead it has turned on us and attacked, robbed, misled, and isolated us.

WALK IN THE TRUTH

We know the truth, and now it is time to walk in it and be set free. It is my prayer that this last chapter will equip you to structure your study of the Word and give you practical and personal applications. I have summarized what I hope will be helpful guidelines in the following six steps:

1. Make the choice not to overreact in anger. Decide to exercise constructive anger. This must be a conscious choice and decision. You must set your heart and mind to change, to turn from your old ways, patterns, and habits and allow the Word of God to transform you. This is not unlike when you made the decision to follow Jesus. The first step is repentance, or turning from one path to another. The children of Israel were given just such a choice: "This day I call heaven and earth as witnesses against you that I have set before you life and death, blessings and curses. Now choose life, so that you and your children may live" (Deut. 30:19 NIV).

At first this will be a deliberate, almost mechanical, decision you'll make in response to each and every situation you encounter that angers or upsets you. For example, we recently moved from Orlando to Colorado. It had been nearly twenty years since I had driven in snow. I was raised in Indiana and had memorized certain responses to driving on ice, but I had forgotten them through lack of use. The first winter that I was out in bad conditions, I temporarily lost control of my car. It was spinning and swerving. Without thinking I heard, *Turn the wheel in the direction of the slide.* What I had learned years ago was brought back to me without any effort on my part, and I was able to bring the car back under control.

2. Allow yourself a chance to step back from what has happened to you before you react. Proverbs 29:20 warns us, "Do you see a man who speaks in haste? There is more hope for a fool than for him" (NIV). I am a student of the Scriptures and have learned that God does not offer much hope to fools. To be effective you must answer the question why. What is it about this encounter or situation that upsets you so much? Is it a control issue? Is it a fear issue? Is this an unresolved hurt issue? Do you feel violated? Often the reason is an obvious one and there is no need to dig deep for the answer, but you still need to regroup before you respond. For example, if one of my children speaks disrespectfully to me I will not like it, but I don't need to figure out why. I do, however, need to carefully choose my response. Being angry and disrespectful in return will not model godliness in their lives. They will only feel justified if I snap back. I need to respond in a way that will help them to realize their behavior is not acceptable and they need to figure out *why* and resolve it. Often this stems from a bad habit. But if my reaction runs deeper than this I must slow down and take a closer look.

3. Take responsibility. Remember, responsibility is a good thing. It is not something to be avoided, but rather embraced. It is the empowerment, ability, or enabling to respond. When you blame others for your reactions, you are reduced to a slave of their whims or actions. Be responsible and own up to both your good and bad responses. First Peter 5:6 exhorts us to "Humble yourselves, therefore, under God's mighty hand, that he may lift you up in due time" (NIV). Humility is an integral part of taking responsibility.

Responsibility and confession go hand in hand. As we discussed earlier, confession means to own up to something, to humbly say it is your fault and resist the ever-present temptation to lay blame on the back of another. Humility deals with your part of the puzzle without worrying about anyone else's reaction. It is

> ❧ *Humility is an integral part of taking responsibility.*

also an abandonment of yourself to God. You are saying, "God, I trust You that if I humble myself, You will lift me out of this situation and set my feet on higher ground."

4. Learn from your mistakes. This is actually a natural progression of taking responsibility. Whenever you take responsibility you are in the position to grow from your mistakes. Proverbs 24:16 encourages us, "For though a righteous man falls seven times, he rises again, but the wicked are brought down by calamity" (NIV). The wicked do not choose to get up; they remain in their fallen state. Their mistakes are not their instructors; they are their downfall. They do not learn from their mistakes; they become entangled and overcome by them. It is not so with the righteous. They humble themselves and grow stronger from each fall.

5. Forgive yourself and others. Forgive those who have hurt you. In Luke 17:4, Jesus told us, "If he sins against you seven times in a day,

> *The righteous humble themselves and grow stronger from each fall.*

and seven times comes back to you and says, 'I repent,' forgive him" (NIV). Forgiveness is to be given to those who repent even if they repeat their offense seven times in one day. We are not in a position to judge them because they have repeated their transgression. Have we not many times repeated our own? We are forgiven the way we forgive. When we don't release others through forgiveness, we find it difficult to release ourselves. When we freely release others we will find it easier to release our own mistakes. But what if they fail to repent? Do we still need to forgive? It is hard to pray, "Forgive us our debts, as we also have forgiven our debtors" (Matt. 6:12 NIV), if we in fact have not forgiven those who have outstanding debts. This debt may well be an owed apology for a previous transgression.

6. Step out of the way and make room for God. When the situation still seems hopeless after you have forgiven and done what is necessary to reconcile, then you are in a position to step back and echo the words of David: "May the LORD judge between you and me. And may the LORD avenge the wrongs you have done to me, but my

> *Freedom is not found in rebellion to God's ways and wisdom.*

hand will not touch you" (1 Sam. 24:12 NIV).

God will accomplish His plan in our lives. We will live in frustration and anger if we think we are ultimately in charge. Rage seeks a target or payment for wrongs done; fury and wrath seek revenge or recompense. But this is an area God does not want us to touch. God's Word tells us, "'It is mine to avenge; I will repay,' and again, 'The Lord will judge his people'" (Heb. 10:30 NIV).

God wants His daughters to be passionate and powerful. If you are not constructive with your anger, if you turn it in on yourself or lash out at those around you, you will lose your passion and become depressed or oppressed. Freedom is not found in rebellion to God's ways and wisdom. Freedom is found when we operate within His life-giving instructions. Then we can live life without regret, without fear, and without dragging along the chains of our past.

Guide to a New Beginning

Here is your chance to live life free from rage and destructive anger—to be passionate and effective, to be compassionate and caring, to take back into control your emotions of anger and frustration. The following is a twenty-one-day Scripture and prayer guide to help you walk in the truths you have learned. You may utilize this in any way you like. You may find areas you wish to concentrate on or revisit for an extended period of time. I have integrated prayer, an opportunity to journal, and Scripture study in an easy, usable, and practical format.

The guide is set up to begin on a Monday. Your day begins with the Morning Moment, introduced by Scripture to help you in the transformation process. Insights of the chosen Scripture are then summarized, followed by prayer. Then you will write your action plan for the day, utilizing the truths you have learned. The Evening Moment gives you the opportunity to note your personal victories (triumphs of the day along with personal sins, mistakes, or failings and confessions). The Mercy List is to note those who have hurt you to whom you are granting mercy. (Note: Once someone is added to your Mercy List, don't take them off.) Write down your actions list for tomorrow in the next section, and then record your thoughts and reflections on your progress today. Some days include a final section called Applying It, which includes thought-provoking exercises. The Sabbath Days

(Days 7, 14, and 21) give you a chance to review the Scriptures from that week and give suggestions of Practical Ideas to Bring It Home.

The entire goal of this book has been transformation, and this only comes by taking up our crosses and denying ourselves. I am not promising you a perfect life at the end of these next few weeks, but if you truly read and apply the Word of God, you will not remain the same. Your heart will soften and become tender again to the things of your Father.

As with anything in the kingdom, it is not how many Scriptures you know but how many you live. The Word is made flesh in your life and therefore produces fruit. Don't skip ahead. This is not a contest or a conquest; it is a process. Some of the Scriptures have already been discussed in previous chapters, but they are worth visiting again. Let's pray and begin this journey!

DAY 1

MORNING MOMENT

Create in me a pure heart, O God, and renew a steadfast spirit within me. Do not cast me from your presence or take your Holy Spirit from me. (Ps. 51:10–11 NIV)

Our adequacy is from God, . . . who also made us adequate as servants of a new covenant, not of the letter, but of the Spirit; for the letter kills, but the Spirit gives life. (2 Cor. 3:5–6 NASB)

Insights

These Scriptures make it glaringly apparent that we will need the Holy Spirit's intervention and instruction if we are to follow in God's ways. In Psalm 51, David cried out for a clean heart and pleaded to remain in God's presence, filled by His Holy Spirit. In John 20 we see that Jesus imparted the Holy Spirit to His disciples. I find it amazing that He equipped them so they could forgive others. Often without the leading of God's spirit we cannot. Second Corinthians 3 points out that it is the Spirit who will equip us, for the Spirit gives life, but the letter kills. We need to invite the Holy Spirit to breathe upon each and every Scripture we encounter that it may bring forth life and transformation.

Heavenly Father,

I come to You in the name of Your precious Son, Jesus. Father, You promised to send the Comforter, the Counselor, the Holy Spirit, to teach me all things and remind me of everything You have said to me. Thank You for this precious gift so that I am not alone as I study Your Word and pursue Your heart. Open my eyes that I might see, my ears that I might hear, and my heart that I might believe.

I now pray according to Your Word, for I am assured it is Your will for my life. Father, create in me a clean heart and renew a right spirit within me.

Cast me not from Your presence, and do not take Your precious Holy Spirit from me. Holy Spirit, I receive Your empowerment to forgive those I need to release. Bring them to my remembrance even now. Let each verse and passage of Scripture be life-giving. I commit to praying before I read and ask for the Spirit in it and not merely the letter of the law. In Jesus' name.

Today I will:

_____

_____

EVENING MOMENT

Triumphs:

_____

_____

Confessions:

_____

_____

Mercy List:

_____

_____

Tomorrow I will:

_____

_____

My thoughts and reflections on the day:

_____

_____

DAY 2

MORNING MOMENT

He who is slow to wrath has great understanding, but he who is impulsive exalts folly. (Prov. 14:29 NKJV)

"In your anger do not sin": Do not let the sun go down while you are still angry, and do not give the devil a foothold. (Eph. 4:26–27 NIV)

Insights

Here the author of Proverbs compared those who are slow to wrath to those with great understanding, and the impulsive, or quick to speak, to a fool. We are to be slow to speak yet quick to resolve our anger. As we have already discovered, part of not sinning in our anger is not to sleep with it. Paul warned us to settle issues in our heart and not allow the devil a foothold or entrance into our life.

Heavenly Father,

I come before You in the name of Jesus. Grant me understanding that I might be slow to wrath. Holy Spirit, check me when I try to fire off an answer quickly. I repent of the times I have been impulsive and foolish. Wash me clean. Help me to go to bed with a clean heart before You. I refuse to sleep with bitterness and anger, and I commit to forgiveness for others as well as for myself. I will not beat myself up as I lie down in my bed. I will not lie down with self-loathing. I ask that You would guard me in the night watches and deliver me from the evil one.

Today I will:

_____

_____

Evening Moment

Triumphs:

_____

_____

Confessions:

_____

_____

Mercy List:

_____

_____

Tomorrow I will:

_____

_____

My thoughts and reflections on the day:

_____

_____

Applying It

When I want to answer impulsively or quickly I will do this
instead (Examples: count to ten, quote a Scripture to myself, be still):

_____

_____

_____

Who am I usually upset with when I lay down my head to go to sleep?

_____

_____

_____

(Make a conscious effort to release these individuals [especially yourself] that you may embrace His mercy in the morning instead of a hangover of bitterness.)

DAY 3

MORNING MOMENT

I said, "I will watch my ways and keep my tongue from sin; I will put a muzzle on my mouth as long as the wicked are in my presence." (Ps. 39:1 NIV)

A fool gives full vent to his anger, but a wise man keeps himself under control. (Prov. 29:11 NIV)

Insights

David certainly understood what it meant to be in the presence of the wicked. Sometimes I imagine it was clearer in his day. Here is David, the king with the heart of a shepherd boy. Rather than fight or defend himself, he chose to muzzle his mouth. This is the very thing Jesus would do generations later. He would remain silent as a lamb before His accusers. This also would apply to joining in with foolish jesting and coarse joking. But often the people we need to muzzle ourselves around are not our enemies and the wicked but the very members of our own house. The Scripture from Proverbs notes that fools vent, but the wise control themselves.

Heavenly Father,

I come to You in the name of Jesus. Forgive the times I have allowed full expression of my anger. Empower me to keep myself under control. I commit to watch my ways and place a muzzle over my mouth when I am in the presence of my enemies. I will keep my tongue from sin and not join in godless conversations.

Today I will:

_____

_____

EVENING MOMENT

Triumphs:

_____

_____

Confessions:

_____

_____

Mercy List:

_____

_____

Tomorrow I will:

_____

_____

My thoughts and reflections on the day:

_____

_____

Applying It

(Pray this prayer, then note your thoughts in the blanks that follow.)
*Lord, show me ways I have been a party to godlessness. I confess the times I
have used my tongue to sin when I was in the company of the unbelievers.
Wash me and help me to use my words to bless others.*

_____

_____

_____

_____

DAY 4

MORNING MOMENT

A gentle answer turns away wrath, but a harsh word stirs up anger. The tongue of the wise commends knowledge, but the mouth of the fool gushes folly. (Prov. 15:1–2 NIV)

Better to dwell in the wilderness, than with a contentious and angry woman. (Prov. 21:19 NKJV)

Insights

I am far from a mealymouthed wife. (I wonder if not too far). But I have learned that during a disagreement with my husband or children or anyone, I can lower the pressure by dropping both the volume and tone of my voice. Harshness only further stirs up the mess. We are often harsh when we are afraid we are not being heard. Then, instead of saying less, we say more until we are gushing foolishness and those around us are identifying with the quote from Proverbs.

Heavenly Father,

I come to You in the name of Jesus. Show me how to be gentle with my responses. I have been harsh in the past, afraid that I was not heard, but I will trust You and gently calm storms with my words instead of further stirring them up. No longer will I allow my mouth to be a geyser but rather a wellspring of life that others may be refreshed instead of drowned or doused by my spray. Lord, forgive me for the times I have been an angry, contentious woman. I choose to be content and peaceful, gentle and meek. I will no longer fight my God-given nature but will yield to my gentler side, knowing it is not the weaker way but the better way.

Today I will:

_____

_____

EVENING MOMENT

Triumphs:

_____

_____

Confessions:

_____

_____

Mercy List:

_____

_____

Tomorrow I will:

_____

_____

My thoughts and reflections on the day:

_____

_____

Applying It

When in the recent past have I answered harshly and things blew up in my face?

_____

_____

When did I answer gently and it calmed a storm?

_____

_____

Do I gush my words or allow them to flow?

_____

_____

Have I been content or contentious?

_____

_____

In what areas am I most contentious?

_____

_____

These are the areas that I am willing to yield to God:

_____

_____

What I am thankful for:

_____

_____

_____

Day 5

Morning Moment

Do not make friends with a hot-tempered man, do not associate with one easily angered, or you may learn his ways and get yourself ensnared. (Prov. 22:24–25 NIV)

A wise man fears the LORD and shuns evil, but a fool is hotheaded and reckless. A quick-tempered man does foolish things, and a crafty man is hated. (Prov. 14:16–17 NIV)

Insights

This is always good advice but even more so now that you are guarding your heart with diligence. Anger and its patterns can be learned or passed on through association with another. Hot-tempered people always seem to have a cause. There is always some point of contention they are wrestling with. If you are not careful you will take up their cause and offense.

Heavenly Father,

I come to You in the name of Jesus. Show me any friends or associates in my life who are easily provoked or quick to anger. I don't want to learn their ways; I want to learn Yours. If I am ensnared in this type of relationship, take the sword of Your Word and cut me free from this entanglement. Lord, I want to fear You and You alone; therefore, I choose to honor You by turning from evil. I want to be childlike, not cunning and crafty. I want to be pliable and conformed to Your image. Hidden in You I will have no fears. Keep me from foolishness by Your holy fear.

Today I will:

_____

_____

Evening Moment

Triumphs:

_____

_____

Confessions:

_____

_____

Mercy List:

_____

Tomorrow I will:

_____

_____

My thoughts and reflections on the day:

_____

_____

Applying It

Are there any hotheaded associates or friends in my life?

_____

_____

What reckless tendencies do I have?

_____

_____

_____

Day 6

Morning Moment

He who guards his mouth and his tongue keeps himself from calamity. (Prov. 21:23 NIV)

Through patience a ruler can be persuaded, and a gentle tongue can break a bone. (Prov. 25:15 NIV)

Insights

When we watch what we say we reap the benefit of protection from adversity, affliction, hardship, and misery. Keeping your mouth is keeping yourself. Through patience or calmness and composure, the rulers in your life can be influenced. Gentle words can break the toughest structure of anyone. It melts away hardness and stiffness.

Heavenly Father,

I come to You in the name of Jesus. I am beginning to realize that I will be more of a woman of influence with gentle words than I ever will be with harsh words. You have promised that these principles work with rulers; how much more will they work with family, friends, and work associates! I yield to Your wisdom and Your ways.

Today I will:

_____

_____

_____

EVENING MOMENT

Triumphs:

_____

_____

Confessions:

_____

_____

Mercy List:

_____

_____

Tomorrow I will:

_____

_____

My thoughts and reflections on the day:

_____

_____

Applying It

How have harsh answers gotten me into trouble in the past?

_____

_____

How can I be more gentle?

_____

_____

Day 7 (Sabbath)

Review the Scriptures for the week and make personal observations:

_____

_____

_____

Practical Ideas to Bring It Home

1. God exhorted the children of Israel to write His word on the doorposts of their homes and hearts. Make signs and put them in the high-traffic areas of your home—not just for your benefit, but for the benefit of others as well.

A dear friend of mine, Tammy, has posted signs around her home that ask the question "Does it honor God?" She has one in her kitchen on her pantry door and in other areas her children frequent. The sign could be anything from a chalkboard message to an embroidered pillow. You can even stencil God's Word on your walls. My son printed a reduced version of Philippians 2:14–15 for our refrigerator door.

2. Another idea is to have a family memory verse that everyone works on for one week (or until they memorize it). Post it in several places and discuss the practical application of it frequently. At breakfast ask your children how they might apply it at school or with friends and family members, and then at dinner discuss it again. Do this until it is in everyone's heart and not just their head. Give them both the directive and the promise. Be careful to emphasize the promises as much as the correction.

3. Enlist the help of a friend in your quest for godliness. Share your heart openly with her. Ask her to hold you accountable in conversation and deed. I recommend having a friend in addition to your husband in this area. The Bible clearly admonishes older women to train younger wives to love their husbands and children.

DAY 8

MORNING MOMENT

Be still before the LORD and wait patiently for him; do not fret when men succeed in their ways, when they carry out their wicked schemes. Refrain from anger and turn from wrath; do not fret—it leads only to evil. (Ps. 37:7–8 NIV)

If anyone considers himself religious and yet does not keep a tight rein on his tongue, he deceives himself and his religion is worthless. (James 1:26 NIV)

Insights

Being still when we are surrounded by what we perceive as injustices is always difficult. But God encourages us not to worry about people who are successful in *their ways*. These are individuals who are enjoying success in their schemes while you wait patiently for God's plan. When we worry it takes us in the direction of evil. The next Scripture states that when we refrain our tongues we testify to the fact that we are trusting God to work on our behalf in our situation.

Heavenly Father,

I come to You in the name of Jesus. I realize I have looked at others and worried. I worried that You were not looking and justice was not served. Forgive my fretting; it has led me only to the evil of judging and comparing myself with others. It has also bred discontent in my life. I will encourage myself in Your Word, and I will sing of Your faithfulness.

Today I will:

_____

_____

EVENING MOMENT

Triumphs:

_____

_____

Confessions:

_____

_____

Mercy List:

_____

_____

Tomorrow I will:

_____

_____

My thoughts and reflections on the day:

_____

_____

Applying It

In what area do I feel the most pressure to judge? Is this an area where I have any responsibility?

_____

_____

I am letting go of these areas of my life, releasing their pressure:

_____

_____

DAY 9

MORNING MOMENT

Finally, all of you, live in harmony with one another; be sympathetic, love as brothers, be compassionate and humble. Do not repay evil with evil or insult with insult, but with blessing, because to this you were called so that you may inherit a blessing. For, "Whoever would love life and see good days must keep his tongue from evil and his lips from deceitful speech." (1 Peter 3:8–10 NIV)

Insights

You are about to inherit something. You will live in harmony and act out of compassion and humility when you don't repay evil or insults with like in turn, but instead bless those who curse you. We have a promise that we are called to inherit a blessing. This blessing comes as a direct result of guarding our tongues and steering clear of deceitful speech. Have you been insulted recently? Then it's time for you to bless the one who cursed you.

Heavenly Father,

I come to You in the name of Jesus. I thank You for the opportunity to inherit a blessing. Impress upon my heart any areas of deceit in my life. Show to me those I have repaid evil with evil. I now choose to bless instead of curse. I will release life instead of death into my life and into the lives of others.

Today I will:

_____

_____

EVENING MOMENT

Triumphs:

_____

_____

Confessions:

_____

_____

Mercy List:

_____

_____

Tomorrow I will:

_____

_____

My thoughts and reflections on the day:

_____

_____

Applying It

When I chose to repay evil for evil what was the outcome?

_____

_____

How was I blessed when I repaid good for evil?

_____

_____

Day 10

An angry man stirs up strife, And a furious man abounds in transgression. (Prov. 29:22 NKJV)

Do not be quickly provoked in your spirit, for anger resides in the lap of fools. (Eccl. 7:9 NIV)

Insights

Angry people keep things stirred up. When you stir something in a pot, it continues to go around and around. The cycle never seems to end as it continues to spin in and out of sight. Issues and offenses that remain unresolved continue in a perpetual state of upheaval. A furious person, someone who is always given to fury, lives with an abundance of transgressions. The Scripture from Ecclesiastes warns against being quickly or easily provoked. I like the imagery we are given here of anger residing or setting up residence in the lap of the foolish. I have four children who have resided on my lap from time to time, especially on airplanes. There was no doubt as to what or who was in my lap.

Heavenly Father,

I come to You in the name of Jesus. I don't ever want to stir up what You would have remain still. I see how my anger has done just this. Forgive me. I don't want anger sitting in my lap. Not only is it uncomfortable, but it is also annoying and obvious to everyone around me. I will slow down my reactions and responses.

Today I will:

_____

_____

EVENING MOMENT

Triumphs:

_____

_____

Confessions:

_____

_____

Mercy List:

_____

_____

Tomorrow I will:

_____

_____

My thoughts and reflections on the day:

_____

_____

Applying It
In what area do I feel continually stirred up?

_____

_____

Day 11

Morning Moment

Do not let any unwholesome talk come out of your mouths, but only what is helpful for building others up according to their needs, that it may benefit those who listen. And do not grieve the Holy Spirit of God, with whom you were sealed for the day of redemption. Get rid of all bitterness, rage and anger, brawling and slander, along with every form of malice. Be kind and compassionate to one another, forgiving each other, just as in Christ God for gave you. (Eph. 4:29–32 NIV)

Insights

This is a mouthful. Notice, it is our responsibility not to allow any unhealthy, injurious, poisonous, or offensive words to escape our lips. This means that it is possible for us to control our mouths; we must carefully choose words that are helpful and edifying to others. We are exhorted to benefit those who hear our words. Words are powerful. They can build or destroy, heal or wound, purify or poison. Not only are we influencing those we see, but there is Someone else who is always present and always listening . . . the Holy Spirit. He is grieved by our lack of restraint and wisdom. He is our very seal for the day of redemption; thus, Paul encouraged us to put away everything that would grieve Him: bitterness, rage, anger, brawling, slander, and every form of malice. *Malice* is defined as "hostility or ill will." It enters with its partner jealousy. These are all fruits of dangerous conditions of the heart.

Heavenly Father,

I come to You in the name of Jesus. Again I submit to the truth that I am to guard my mouth. I also realize that the meditations of my heart often guide the words of my mouth. Make the motives of my heart clean and acceptable in Your sight. Quicken in me a sensitivity to the ears of those around me and to the grieving of Your Holy Spirit. May my words hold the

*power of healing, health, and wisdom. May they empower the hearers to
serve You and love You in a deeper and truer way. In obedience to Your
Word, I rid myself of the fruit of malice. Give me Your eyes and the compassion to forgive as You have so graciously and generously forgiven me.*

Today I will:

_____

_____

Evening Moment

Triumphs:

_____

_____

Confessions:

_____

_____

Mercy List:

_____

_____

Tomorrow I will:

_____

_____

My thoughts and reflections on the day:

_____

_____

Applying It

What wholesome words can I speak to counteract the unwholesome? (Write down some blessings and speak them to the appropriate individuals.)

_____

_____

_____

_____

_____

_____

_____

_____

_____

DAY 12

MORNING MOMENT

A wise man's heart guides his mouth, and his lips promote instruction. Pleasant words are a honeycomb, sweet to the soul and healing
to the bones. There is a way that seems right to a man, but in the end
it leads to death. (Prov. 16:23–25 NIV)

Better a patient man than a warrior, a man who controls his temper
than one who takes a city. (Prov. 16:32 NIV)

Insights

Here we have another confirmation of the connection between
the heart and the mouth. There is an unseen but intertwined relationship. The wise allow their hearts—not their feelings, wrong habit
patterns, emotions, or reactions—to determine their words and
actions. Lips that inspire instruction or learning are mindful of how
words affect others. Their conversation guides others toward righteousness. Their words are sweet and leave a pleasant rather than a bitter taste in the mouths of others. Our second reference from Proverbs
exalts the strength of the patient over that of the warrior. Warriors
have lightning-fast responses. But the patient are more in control and
more powerful than warriors. Then the proverb pushes the comparison further: A man or a woman in control of his or her temper is
mightier than one who takes a city. A single man who has mastered
his temper is superior to a single warrior who conquers a city. Most of
us would find the conquest of a city much more impressive than the
mastery of a temper, but God does not. He understands that the wars
that rage within often dwarf the wars that rage without.

Heavenly Father,
I come to You in the name of Jesus. I want my heart to rule my mouth.
No longer will I give my emotions the reins to my life. Holy Spirit, I

171

bow to Your place of preeminence in my life. I want to speak Your pleasant words that I might experience healing as well as add health and instruction to those who hear and dine upon my words. Give me the revelation of the importance of words. I realize they enter us as nothing else can. I want to inspire instruction and godliness in my life as well as in the lives of others. I turn from the path that seems right to me and turn to Your path for life. Let me exemplify the strength found in controlling my temper. I want to be mighty in the sight of God not in the sight of men.

Today I will:

_____

_____

EVENING MOMENT

Triumphs:

_____

_____

Confessions:

_____

_____

Mercy List:

_____

_____

Tomorrow I will:

_____

_____

My thoughts and reflections on the day:

_____

_____

_____

Applying It
(Pray this prayer)
Father, show me who needs healthy words.

DAY 13

MORNING MOMENT

Live in harmony with one another. Do not be proud, but be willing to associate with people of low position. Do not be conceited. Do not repay anyone evil for evil. Be careful to do what is right in the eyes of everybody. If it is possible, as far as it depends on you, live at peace with everyone. Do not take revenge, my friends, but leave room for God's wrath, for it is written: "It is mine to avenge; I will repay," says the Lord. (Rom. 12:16–19 NIV)

Insights

To live in harmony is to live in a way that is compatible, in tune, and in friendship with others. We are to lay aside any distinction we may think we possess and fellowship with those of low position. There is a warning against conceit, which is self-admiration or arrogance, an overawe with oneself. Remember, in Christ we are to embrace the nature of a servant to one another. When we lay aside arrogance and pride, we will not repay evil with evil, we will turn the other cheek. We are exhorted to go to great lengths to do right for the sake of others and, as far as it concerns us, to live in peace with *everyone*. This means we will withhold our hand from revenge and in faith and childlike trust step aside and make room for God's justice. He alone knows all sides and is faithful and ever true.

Heavenly Father,

I come to You in the name of Jesus. Show me how to be a friend to those You bring across my path. Open my eyes to any and every area of prejudice I may have hidden in my heart. Give me the revelation of a servant in both word and deed. I am not my own; You hold my life in Your hand. I trust You to protect me. I will not repay evil with evil, for You gave me good when I deserved evil. I lay aside the faulty armor of pride and arrogance. I don't want to be a stumbling block to anyone. Holy

Spirit, guard my steps that I might not sin against You. I lay aside the yoke of pride and fear and take up the mantle of humility and faith in Your goodness.

Today I will:

_____

_____

Evening Moment

Triumphs:

_____

_____

Confessions:

_____

_____

Mercy List:

_____

_____

Tomorrow I will:

_____

_____

My thoughts and reflections on the day:

_____

_____

Applying It

I let go of vengeance with _____ and transfer them to my Mercy List.

(Pray this prayer)

Father, expose areas of prejudice in my life.

Day 14 (Sabbath)

Review the Scriptures from this week, and make personal observations:

_____

_____

_____

Practical Ideas to Bring It Home

1. Start a prayer group for mothers, wives, or just friends. Make it a safe place where each person can feel open and honest about their fears and flaws. Pray for others that you might be healed.

2. Take walks while listening to praise or worship tapes or other Christian music that lifts your spirit and draws you closer to His presence.

3. Let go of the lie of perfection. Decide what is really important to you and let the other things go. This will reduce a lot of areas of pressure in your life that you may not even be aware of.

DAY 15

MORNING MOMENT

My soul will be satisfied as with the richest of foods; with singing lips my mouth will praise you. On my bed I remember you; I think of you through the watches of the night. Because you are my help, I sing in the shadow of your wings. My soul clings to you; your right hand upholds me. (Ps. 63:5–8 NIV)

He will cover you with his feathers, and under his wings you will find refuge; his faithfulness will be your shield and rampart. (Ps. 91:4 NIV)

Insights

Think of the sensation after you've attended a banquet. One where you sampled a vast array of delicious and delicate foods, but didn't overdo it. Each food was presented beautifully and you enjoyed just enough and not too much. You are satisfied and slip into a relaxed, almost dreamlike state of contentment. We are invited to taste and see that the Lord is good. Instead of lying down in anger or frustration over the events of our day, our soul is invited to experience dessert. We are exhorted to lie down and think about our Father, to snuggle in tight under His wings of protection. We are given the visual imagery of a mighty bird with its young sheltered in the warmth and downy protection of its wings. Separated from the world for the evening, this is a haven from every storm or enemy. In this atmosphere we can sing of the Lord's help and protection in our life. Every day can be a celebration of Him.

Sleep is a mysterious state. It is a time when we are truly the most vulnerable. We lose our consciousness and slip away to another place and time for a few hours. Children tend to sleep more deeply than adults do. Content and carefree, they trade the activities of their day for the surrender of the night. As adults our slumber is not always the time of rest it was when we were children. Too often we bring the activities of our day to bed with us. We wrestle worries and fears until the break of dawn and often wake wearier than when we lay down. Sleep does not restore or satisfy us; it leaves us heavy and groggy. Sleep is so important to our emotional and physical well-being. Without the proper amount of rest, we will find it extremely difficult to function. I found I never slept well when I punished myself before going to bed. So on our beds we should turn our eyes from ourselves and, instead, behold Him. He will keep us safe as we trust in Him and rest at night.

Heavenly Father,

I come to You in the name of Jesus. As I lie down to rest, let me feast on Your faithfulness. If I wake during the night, do not let the cares of my day overwhelm me but let meditations of You cover me in downy softness. I claim Your promises in the night watches. I release fear and cling to you as an infant clings to his mother. Change my sleep from tossing turmoil to refreshing rest. I trust in You and Your protection and refuse to worry about tomorrow.

Today I will:

_____

_____

EVENING MOMENT

Triumphs:

_____

_____

Confessions:

_____

_____

Mercy List:

_____

_____

Tomorrow I will:

_____

_____

My thoughts and reflections on the day:

_____

_____

Applying It

(Write down one attribute of God. Now pick out praise music and
sing it during the day and rejoice over this attribute of the Father.)

_____

Day 16

Morning Moment

Be merciful to me, O God, be merciful to me! For my soul trusts in You; And in the shadow of Your wings I will make my refuge, Until these calamities have passed by. (Ps. 57:1 NKJV)

Insights

So many are excited about angelic protection, but do you know that David was talking about finding his refuge under God's wings? We will fight anger when we have not developed our trust in God. I learned long ago that I cannot protect myself—only God can protect me. He is the One we must run to. When you are frustrated, falsely accused, slandered, or just plain lied about, run to the refuge of His wings. Do not allow the enemy to trap you into defending or attempting to protect yourself; you cannot. God invites us to hide ourselves in Him until the storms of life have passed. This protection is provided not by any act of our own merit but because *He* is faithful even when we are faithless. He is merciful, therefore we must go to Him in like manner. Rage cannot abide in the shadow of His wings—there is no place for it there. Rage is never a refuge, though it will lie and say it is. It must be laid aside in order to enter into God's presence.

Heavenly Father,

I come to You in the name of Jesus. Allow Your Holy Spirit to impress the image of Your protection deep within my soul. I want to hide in You as the calamities of life come and go. Because I need mercy, I extend mercy before entering the refuge of Your presence. I will not foolishly trust in myself or in man, but I will allow my soul to trust only in You.

Today I will:

_____

_____

EVENING MOMENT

Triumphs:

_____

_____

Confessions:

_____

Mercy List:

_____

_____

Tomorrow I will:

_____

My thoughts and reflections on the day:

_____

_____

Applying It
In which areas am I desiring God's protection?

_____

_____

DAY 17

When words are many, sin is not absent, but he who holds his tongue is wise. The tongue of the righteous is choice silver, but the heart of the wicked is of little value. The lips of the righteous nourish many, but fools die for lack of judgment. (Prov. 10:19–21 NIV)

Do not be quick with your mouth, do not be hasty in your heart to utter anything before God. God is in heaven and you are on earth, so let your words be few. (Eccl. 5:2 NIV)

Insights:

Have you ever experienced a phone call or conversation that started out just fine but then took a turn for the worse? I have often wondered if it is a time factor issue. What begins as godly too often regresses with the passage of time or words. Some of us just need to shorten our time on the phone. When we cannot see whom we are talking to or whom we are talking about, we often fail to use discretion in our words. Better to change subjects frequently than dwell on one too long and say things you will only regret later. Choice silver is not common but refined by fire. When we allow the fire of God's Word to purify our conversation, we will find the impurities and indiscretions removed from our conversation. We are admonished to be slow with our mouths, to weigh what we say before we just blurt it out onto the table for others to dine on. A quick mouth represents a hasty heart. When we come before God, we are to be of few words. He is in heaven while we are merely earthbound inhabitants. An integral part of the proper fear or respect of God is to know when to speak and when to listen. We learn by listening, not speaking, so be still and know that He is God.

Heavenly Father,

I come to You in the name of Jesus. Cause me to inventory and weigh my words. Let each of them be potent and powerful and not vain and idle. Holy Spirit, reveal the relationships where I fall into this snare and let me now be an example of godliness instead of foolishness. I want my words to inspire, instruct, and bless others. Create in me a greater awareness and sense of value when it comes to my conversation.

Today I will:

_____

_____

EVENING MOMENT

Triumphs:

Confessions:

_____

Mercy List:

_____

_____

Tomorrow I will:

_____

_____

My thoughts and reflections on the day:

_____

_____

Applying It
In what types of situations and with whom do I talk too much?

_____

_____

What relationships am I fearful about?

_____

_____

Day 18

A fool's mouth is his undoing, and his lips are a snare to his soul. The words of a gossip are like choice morsels; they go down to a man's inmost parts. (Prov. 18:7–8 NIV)

A man who lacks judgment derides his neighbor, but a man of understanding holds his tongue. A gossip betrays a confidence, but a trustworthy man keeps a secret. (Prov. 11:12–13 NIV)

Insights

Enough said about the fool and his mouth. Now let's look at the words of a gossip. They are described as choice morsels, delicious to the taste but costly to the soul. As you listen, you find yourself wanting to hear more. You convince yourself that you can handle what you're hearing; after all, you're mature and wise . . . you'll remain unbiased. What you don't realize is, your well has been poisoned. The next time you see the discussed person or merely hear her name you feel a pressure to judge her, not her actions but her motives. What does this have to do with personal anger? Rage and gossip share a common root: fear. Both are exercised in a futile attempt at self-protection (I say futile, for only God can truly protect us). Gossip is always a betrayal of trust. One person is sold out for the security, position, or influence of another. Your heart has been tenderized, and when you talk about another or listen to someone else as they pass on information, you should feel a check. If the enemy knows you are zealously guarding what goes out of your mouth, he might try to trip you up with what goes in your ears. The Bible tells us the wicked listen to a gossip (Prov. 17:4). You must guard your heart with all diligence, for it is the very source of your life in Christ.

Heavenly Father,
  I come before You in the name of Jesus. Show me how to guard my

ears as well as my heart. Separate the precious from the vile in my life that I might not sin against You in my form of conversation. Place a guard over my ears as well and anoint me with wisdom to speak in these situations as they may arise. I will allow no one to speak ill of those close to me. I will cover them with prayer, love, and Your Word.

Today I will:

_____

_____

EVENING MOMENT

Triumphs:

_____

_____

Confessions:

_____

_____

Mercy List:

_____

_____

Tomorrow I will:

_____

_____

My thoughts and reflections on the day:

_____

_____

Day 19

He who guards his lips guards his life, but he who speaks rashly will come to ruin. (Prov. 13:3 NIV)

He who loves a pure heart and whose speech is gracious will have the king for his friend. (Prov. 22:11 NIV)

A man's belly shall be satisfied with the fruit of his mouth; and with the increase of his lips shall he be filled. Death and life are in the power of the tongue: and they that love it shall eat the fruit thereof. (Prov. 18:20–21 KJV)

Insights

We cannot get away from the connection between anger and the mouth as well as the lips and the heart. The abundance or contents of our heart are revealed by the conversations of our lips. In my estimation Proverbs 13 contains the sum total of this wisdom. In our present culture the power of anyone's words has been downplayed. For someone to give their word on something means nothing anymore. To counter this we have contracts that lawyers make fortunes getting their clients out of. God does not offer us a contract but a covenant of promise based on His name and Word. He is not a man that He should lie. He is the faithful and true witness. Heaven and earth will pass away, but His Word will endure forever. If we honor His Word with our obedience and faith, He will honor us with transformation. There is the saying that you are what you eat. Feast upon the truth of God's words and you cannot remain the same. It will turn you into a friend of the King.

Heavenly Father,

I come to You in the name of Jesus. Thank You that You have spread a banquet table of goodness and mercy before me and have bid me to come and eat freely from Your hand. May I in turn feast on the good and pleasant and not the harmful and destructive. Father, forgive me and wash me clean of all iniquity I have sown in the area of my speech and through anger in my actions. With all my heart my deepest desire is to be one who brings pleasure to You. I want to be a faithful friend to You because You have always been faithful to me. I turn from the fruit of death and embrace Your paths in life.

Today I will:

_____

_____

EVENING MOMENT

Triumphs:

_____

_____

Confessions:

_____

_____

Mercy List:

_____

_____

Tomorrow I will:

_____

_____

My thoughts and reflections on the day:

_____

_____

Applying It
What kind of friend do I want?

_____

_____

What kind of friend am I?

_____

_____

Day 20

It is God who works in you to will and to act according to his good purpose. *Do everything without complaining or arguing, so that you may become blameless and pure, children of God without fault in a crooked and depraved generation, in which you shine like stars in the universe as you hold out the word of life*—in order that I may boast on the day of Christ that I did not run or labor for nothing. (Phil. 2:13–16 NIV, emphasis added)

To him who is able to keep you from falling and to present you before his glorious presence without fault and with great joy—to the only God our Savior be glory, majesty, power and authority, through Jesus Christ our Lord, before all ages, now and forevermore! Amen. (Jude 24–25 NIV)

Insights

When we do not complain or argue, we afford ourselves the opportunity to experience a shining transformation. Though this present world may be filled with depravity and perverseness, darkness cannot shroud or overcome our light. Look up at the stars of this universe—they punctuate a sky of darkness with such beauty that on a clear and starry night it is never the darkness we notice but the small beacons of hope that pierce it. When God looks down at this creation of darkness, it is the light of His children that He notices. Hold high the lamp of His Word and shine it forth as a beacon of hope and truth for generations to follow.

These two verses are some of John's and my favorites. God is truly faithful to keep us from falling. He will uphold us by His Word of truth and present us with great joy as faultless. There is no mention of shame. He is not looking for reason to reject or condemn us. These already existed; therefore He sent His Son. His promise remains now and forevermore! It is for those near and far . . . it is for you. Tremble in the joy of it, grab it with your heart, and you will never be the same.

✎ Heavenly Father,

I come to You in the name of Jesus. I will look at the stars and believe You see Your light in me, not my darkness. Your Word will light any area of darkness; it is the lamp that shines upon my path. I turn from the foolishness of my own counsel, from the light of my own reasoning. I believe that this book and these truths have come into my life that I might walk in Your light. I thank You for this time of transformation. Be glorified in my life. In every relationship and in all I do may those around me witness Your work in my life.

Today I will:

_____

_____

EVENING MOMENT

Triumphs:

_____

_____

Confessions:

_____

_____

Mercy List:

_____

_____

Tomorrow I will:

_____

_____

My thoughts and reflections on the day:

_____

_____

Applying It
What good things do I see in myself?

_____

_____

How have I grown?

_____

_____

Day 21 (Sabbath)

Review the Scriptures for this week, and make personal observations:

_____

_____

_____

Practical Ideas to Bring It Home

1. Get enough rest, fresh air, and sunshine. Celebrate and be thankful for God's creation.

2. Eat candlelight dinners with your children. It has a calming effect on them just as it does on you.

3. Get rid of things that breed discontentment in your life. Dump catalogs in the garbage can unless you really intend to order from them. Only get magazines that inspire and do not depress you. Be thankful for what you have and do not covet.

Epilogue

At this point, if you have read everything with an open heart and gone through the three weeks of renewing your mind, you are not the same person who began this book. Exposure to the Word of God in such a concentrated level of study cannot help but change you. This change, of course, began on the inside and will work its way out. I am sure this encounter with truth has not been altogether pain-free for you. Often great change comes at the expense of great pain. My encounter with truth was painful but it was not pain without purpose. I was encouraged by the fact God carefully trains and disciplines His children.

> And you have forgotten the exhortation which speaks to you as to sons: "My son, do not despise the chastening of the Lord, nor be discouraged when you are rebuked by Him; For whom the Lord loves He chastens, and scourges every son whom He receives." If you endure chastening, God deals with you as with sons; for what son is there whom a father does not chasten? (Hebrews 12:5–7 NKJV)

You have taken some brave and courageous steps. You have dared to face an area of darkness in your life. You have cracked the door of your heart and allowed the light of God's Word to expose and heal areas of unresolved anger. Too many marriages, relationships, and families end up divided and torn due to unresolved anger. It is my prayer that God will honor the steps you have taken and that your past will once and forever be left behind you. Vow to never revisit those ruins of destruction again. Take this promise of God and hide it in your heart:

> Now to Him who is able to keep you from stumbling, and to present you faultless before the presence of His glory with exceeding joy, to God our Savior, Who alone is wise, be glory and majesty, dominion and power, both now and forever. (Jude 1:24–25 NKJV)

We will never be perfect, but He is. Even when we are faithless, He is faithful. When we are weak, He is strong. Labor in the empowering grace of God and do not return to the frailty of your own strength.

To receive JBM's free newsletter, *The Messenger*, and to receive a free color catalog of ministry resources, please contact:

John Bevere Ministries

UNITED STATES
PO Box 888
Palmer Lake, CO 80133-0888
800-648-1477 (US & Canada)
Tel: 719-487-3000
Fax: 719-487-3300
E-mail: jbm@johnbevere.org
Web site: www.johnbevere.org

EUROPE & AFRICA
PO Box 2794
Walsall
WS2 7YQ
UNITED KINGDOM
Tel: 44 (0) 870-745-5790
Fax: 44 (0) 970-745-5791
E-mail: jbmeurope@johnbevere.org
Web site: www.johnbevere.org.uk

AUSTRALIA
PO Box 6200
Dural CD NSW 2158
AUSTRALIA

The Messenger television program airs on the God Digital Network in Europe and the Australian Christian Channel. Please check your local listings for day and time.

nur✝ure

Give and Get What You Need to Flourish

Curriculum coming soon!

Fight Like *a Girl*
The Power of Being a Woman

You are an answer, not a problem.

Curriculum Includes

12 - 30 Minute Sessions on 4 DVDs
Hardback Book and Interactive Workbook
Makeup Bag
Bracelet - Genuine Swarovski Austrian Crystal
Advertising Poster

Why is it that women often don't like women? What could possibly cause a large portion of us to reject our own gender? More often than not we lack an appreciation for women. We associate men with strength and women with weakness. We therefore attempt life in roles as men, only to find ourselves conflicted. But God is awakening and empowering His daughters to realize who they truly are, as well as their unique and significant contributions.

KISSED
THE GIRLS
AND MADE
THEM CRY

Kit Includes

4 Sessions on 2 DVDs
Bonus Q&A
Best-Selling Book
Interactive Workbook
Advertising Poster

Don't believe the lie—sexual purity isn't about rules...it's about freedom and power. It is time to take back what we've cheaply given away. The *Kissed the Girls and Made Them Cry* kit is not only designed for youth but also for women of all ages who long for a greater intimacy with Jesus and need to embrace God's healing and restoring love.

"I'm 15. and through your kit my nightmare has been turned back to a dream!"